ERVING GOFFMAN

ENCOUNTERS

Two Studies in the Sociology
of Interaction

ALLEN LANE
THE PENGUIN PRESS

Copyright © The Bobbs-Merrill Company, Inc., 1961

First published in the United States of America in 1961
by The Bobbs-Merrill Company, Inc.
First published in Great Britain in 1972

Allen Lane The Penguin Press
74 Grosvenor Street, London W1

ISBN 0 7139 0314 7

Printed in Great Britain by
Hazell Watson & Viney Ltd, Aylesbury, Bucks
Set in Monotype Times Roman

CONTENTS

PREFACE

The study of every unit of social organization must eventually lead to an analysis of the interaction of its elements. The analytical distinction between units of organization and processes of interaction is, therefore, not destined to divide up our work for us. A division of labor seems more likely to come from distinguishing among types of units, among types of elements, or among types of processes.

Sociologists have traditionally studied face-to-face interaction as part of the area of 'collective behavior'; the units of social organization involved are those that can form by virtue of a breakdown in ordinary social intercourse: crowds, mobs, panics, riots. The other aspect of the problem of face-to-face interaction – the units of organization in which orderly and uneventful face-to-face interaction occurs – has been neglected until recently, although there is some early work on classroom interaction, topics of conversation, committee meetings, and public assemblies.

Instead of dividing face-to-face interaction into the eventful and the routine, I propose a different division – into *unfocused interaction* and *focused interaction*. Unfocused interaction consists of those interpersonal communications that result solely by virtue of persons being in one another's presence, as when two strangers across the room from each other check up on each other's clothing, posture, and general manner, while each modifies his own demeanor because he himself is under observation. Focused interaction occurs when people effectively agree to sustain for a time a single focus of cognitive and visual attention, as in a conversation, a board game, or a joint task sustained by a close face-to-face circle of contributors. Those sustaining together a single focus of attention will, of course, engage one another in focused interaction, too. They will not do so in their capacity as participants in the focused activity, however, and persons present who are not in the focused activity will equally participate in this unfocused interaction.

The two papers in this volume are concerned with focused interaction only. I call the natural unit of social organization in which focused interaction occurs a *focused gathering*, or an *encounter*, or a *situated activity system*. I assume that instances of this natural unit have enough in common to make it worthwhile to study them as a type. Three different terms are used out of desperation rather than by design; as will be suggested, each of the three in its own way is unsatisfactory, and each is satisfactory in a way that the others are not. The two essays deal from different points of view with this single unit of social organization. The first paper, 'Fun in Games', approaches focused gatherings from an examination of the kind of games that are played around a table. The second paper, 'Role Distance', approaches focused gatherings through a review and criticism of social-role analysis.

The study of focused gatherings has been greatly stimulated recently by the study of group psychotherapy and especially by 'small-group analysis'. I feel, however, that full use of this work is impeded by a current tendency to identify focused gatherings too easily with social groups.[1] A small but interesting area of study is thus obscured by the biggest title, 'social group', that can be found for it. Some prefatory comments on this definitional issue can serve as an introduction to the unit of social organization to be considered in this book.

Focused gatherings and groups do share some properties and even some that are requisites. If persons are to come together into a focused gathering and stay for a time, then certain 'system problems' will have to be solved: the participants will have to submit to rules of recruitment, to limits on overt hostility, and to some division of labor. Such requisites are also found in social groups. Now if social groups and focused gatherings both exhibit the same set of properties, what is the use of distinguishing between these two units of social organization? And would not this distinction become especially unnecessary when all the members of the group are the only participants in the gathering?

Paradoxically, the easier it is to find similarities between these two units, the more mischief may be caused by not distinguishing between them. Let us address the problem, then: what is the difference between a group and a focused gathering?

A social group may be defined as a special type of social organization. Its elements are individuals: they perceive the organization as a

1. For a well-stated argument that encounters and groups are the same, see E. F. Borgatta and L. S. Cottrell, Jr, 'On the Classification of Groups', *Sociometry*, 18 (1955), pp. 416–18.

distinct collective unit, a social entity, apart from the particular relationships the participants may have to one another; they perceive themselves as members who belong, identifying with the organization and receiving moral support from doing so; they sustain a sense of hostility to outgroups. A symbolization of the reality of the group and one's relation to it is also involved.

Small groups, according to this conception of groups, are distinguished by what their size makes possible (although not necessary), such as extensive personal knowledge of one another by the members, wide consensus, and reliance on informal role differentiation. Small groups themselves – let me temporarily call them 'little groups' to distinguish them from all the other phenomena studied under the title of small-group research – differ in the degree to which they are formally or informally organized; long-standing or short-lived; multibonded or segmental; relatively independent, as in the case of some families and gangs, or pinned within a well-bounded organizational structure, as in the case of army platoons or office cliques.

Social groups, whether big or little, possess some general organizational properties. These properties include regulation of entering and leaving; capacity for collective action; division of labor, including leadership roles; socialization function, whether primary or adult; a means of satisfying personal ends; and latent and manifest social function in the environing society. These same properties, however, are also found in many other forms of social organization, such as a social relationship binding two persons, a network of relationships interlocking a set of friends, a complex organization, or a set of businessmen or gamesters who abide by ground rules while openly concerned only with defeating the designs of their coparticipants. It is possible, of course, to call any social relationship between two individuals a two-person group, but I think this is unwise. A group that is just beginning or dying may have only two members, but I feel that the conceptual framework with which this ill-manned group is to be studied ought to differ from the framework used in studying the many-sidedness of the social relationship between these two individuals. And to call any two individuals a 'two-person group' solely because there is a social relationship between them is to slight what is characteristic of groups and to fail to explore what is uniquely characteristic of relationships.

Little groups are not difficult to find, and while they are usually studied in their natural setting, they can be created for purposes of study.[2] Persons who agree to participate for a year in weekly sessions of a group-psychotherapy meeting are likely, during the year, to come to constitute a little group. A set of persons herded into an observation room and required to work together on a predesigned face-to-face task, sometimes under instruction as to how well they are likely to get along, can give rise to a little group of a sort, especially if a long series of trials is run. Even a few passing strangers huddled for a moment's conversation on the street and showing willingness to maintain orderly face-to-face interaction can be described as a fugitive and trivial 'ad hoc' group, a group that has not been influenced by previous contacts of the members, there having been none, nor influencing future interaction among members, because none is likely to occur.

In the case of laboratory and ad hoc gatherings, a pale and limited version of the attributes of little groups may be uncovered. The issue, however, is not the triviality and limitation of these data as samplings of little-group life – for trivial examples examined under conditions of experimental control ought to be useful to investigators. It is that the researcher is often studying processes characteristic of focused interaction[3], rather than groups as such. (A laboratory experiment that provides severely limited data about little groups can nevertheless provide substantial data concerning face-to-face interaction processes. Thus, I am not arguing for a distinction between natural and experimental studies but between groups, natural or experimental, and gatherings, natural or experimental.)

Given these definitions, differences between groups and encounters become apparent. Some of the properties that are important to focused gatherings or encounters, taken as a class, seem much less important to little groups, taken as a class. Examples of such properties include embarrassment, maintenance of poise, capacity for nondistractive verbal communication, adherence to a code regarding giving up and taking over the speaker role, and allocation of spatial position. Furthermore, a crucial attribute of focused gatherings – the participant's maintenance of continuous engrossment in the official

2. Perhaps the most notable study of this kind is Muzafer Sherif and C. W. Sherif, *Groups in Harmony and Tension* (New York: Harper, 1953).

3. A similar argument is presented by Hans Zetterberg in 'Compliant Actions', *Acta Sociologica*, 2 (1957), pp. 179–201, especially p. 183, from which I quote: 'What is important to us here is to note that most laboratory experiments on small groups are experiments with action systems. They are usually *not* experiments with "social groups" in the complex sense in which sociologists use this term.'

focus of activity – is not a property of social groups in general, for most groups, unlike encounters, continue to exist apart from the occasions when members are physically together. A coming-together can be merely a phase of group life; a falling-away, on the other hand, is the end of a particular encounter, even when the same pattern of interaction and the same participants appear at a future meeting. Finally, there are many gatherings – for example, a set of strangers playing poker in a casino – where an extremely full array of inter-action processes occurs with only the slightest development of a sense of group. All these qualifications can be made even though data for the study of little groups and for the study of focused gatherings are likely to be drawn from the same social occasion. In the same way, these qualifications can be made even though any social group can be partly described in terms of the character of the gatherings its members maintain together, just as any gathering can be described in terms of the overlapping group affiliations of its participants.[4]

In the life of many little groups, occasions regularly arise when all the members and only the members come together and jointly sustain a situated activity system or encounter: they hold a meeting, play a game, discuss a movie, or take a cigarette break together. To call these gatherings 'meetings of the group' can easily entrap one into think-ing that one is studying the group directly. Actually, these are meetings of persons who are members of a group, and, even though the meet-ing may have been called because of issues faced by the group, the initial data concern participants in a meeting, not members of a group.

It is true that on such occasions there is likely to be a correspon-dence between the realm of group life and the realm of face-to-face interaction process. For example, leadership of a little group may be expressed during gatherings of members by the question of who is chairman, or who talks the most, or who is most frequently addressed. It is also likely that the leadership demonstrated in the gathering will both influence, and be influenced by, the leadership in the group. But group leadership is not made up exclusively of an 'averaging' of posi-tions assumed during various gatherings. In fact, the group may face circumstances in which its leader is careful to let others take leader-ship during a meeting, his capacity to lead the group resting upon the tactful way in which he plays a minor role during gatherings of group members. The group leader can do this because 'taking the chair' is intrinsically a possibility of gatherings, not groups.

4. For this and many other suggestions, I am very grateful to Hanan Selvin.

Similarly, the factions that occur in a little group may coincide with the coalitions formed during gatherings of group members. We know, however, that such 'open' expression of structural cleavage can be seen as dangerous to the group and destructive of the opportunity of accomplishing business during the gathering, so that this congruence will often specifically be avoided. Coalitions during the gathering will then crosscut factions in the group.

Further, even when all the members of a group are the only participants in a gathering, and the gathering has been called in order to transact business pertaining to the group, we will inevitably find that the persons present are also members of other social groups and that each of these groups can claim only a sub-set – moreover a different sub-set – of those present. Some of the positions in the gathering are likely to be allocated on the basis of these divisive group affiliations. Of course, other positions in the gathering are likely to be allocated on the basis of factors other than group affiliation, e.g., recognized experience, command of language, priority of appearance in the meeting place, or age.

Finally, while the morale of the group and the solidarity of its members may increase with an increasing number of meetings, there are strong groups that rarely have focused gatherings containing all their members and weak groups that have many.

There are issues apart from those that arise because of the difference between being a member of a group and being a participant in a gathering. Some of the properties that clearly belong both to groups and to gatherings turn out upon close examination to mean two different ranges of things, in part because of a difference in level of abstraction employed in the two cases. For example, one form of leadership that can be extremely important in gatherings is the maintenance of communication ground rules, i.e., 'order'; this aspect of leadership does not seem to have the same importance in group analysis, however. Similarly, tension-management is a requirement in both groups and gatherings, but what is managed in each case seems different. Tension in encounters arises when the official focus of attention is threatened by distractions of various kinds; this state of uneasiness is managed by tactful acts, such as the open expression in a usable way of what is distracting attention. There will be circumstances, then, when tactfully expressed ranklings may ease interaction in a gathering while destroying the group to which the participants happen to belong.

The preceding arguments are meant to suggest that a frequent empirical congruence between the structure of a group and the structure of a gathering of its members does not imply any invariant analytical relation between the two realms. The concepts tailored to the study of groups and those tailored to the study of encounters may be analytically related, but these relations are by no means self-evident.

I want to say, finally, that distinguishing between little groups and focused gatherings allows one not only to see that a gathering may itself generate a fleeting little group but also to examine the relation between this group and long-standing groups from which the participants in the encounter may derive.

When all and only the members of a little group come together in a gathering, the effect of the gathering, depending on the outcome of its activity, will be to strengthen or weaken somewhat the little group. The potentiality of the encounter for generating its own group seems to be expended in what it does for and to the long-standing group. Often, there seems to be no chance for the fleeting circle of solidarity to develop much solidity of its own, for it fits too well in a pattern already established. However, when individuals come into a gathering who are not also members of the same little group, and especially if they are strangers possessing no prior relationships to one another, then the group formation that is fostered by the encounter will stand out as a contrast to all other groups of which the encounter's participants are members. It is under these circumstances – when the participants in a gathering have not been together in a group before and are not likely to be so again – that the locally generated group seems to cast its strongest shadow. It is under these circumstances, too, that the fate of these two units of organization seems most closely tied together, the effectiveness of the gathering rather directly affecting the solidarity of the group.

Paradoxically, then, if a gathering, on its own, is to generate a group and have group-formation mark the gathering as a memorable event, then a stranger or two may have to be invited – and this is sometimes carefully done on sociable occasions. These persons anchor the group-formation that occurs, preventing it from drifting back into the relationships and groups that existed previously among the participants.

FUN IN GAMES[1]

1. I am grateful to the Center for the Integration of Social Science Theory of the University of Calfornia, Berkeley, and to the Society for the Study of Human Ecology, New York, for support during the preparation of this paper.

MIRABELL *and* FAINALL [*rising from cards*]

MIRABELL: *You are a fortunate man, Mr Fainall.*
FAINALL: *Have we done?*
MIRABELL: *What you please. I'll play on to entertain you.*
FAINALL: *No, I'll give you your revenge another time, when you are not so indifferent; you are thinking of something else now, and play too negligently; the coldness of a losing gamester lessens the pleasure of the winner. I'd no more play with a man that slighted his ill fortune, than I'd make love to a woman who undervalued the loss of her reputation.*

– William Congreve, *The Way of the World*

INTRODUCTION

1. *Play and Seriousness*. In daily life, games are seen as part of recreation and 'in principle devoid of important repercussions upon the solidity and continuity of collective and institutional life'.[2] Games can be fun to play, and fun alone is the approved reason for playing them. The individual, in contrast to his treatment of 'serious' activity, claims a right to complain about a game that does not pay its way in immediate pleasure and, whether the game is pleasurable or not, to plead a slight excuse, such as an indisposition of mood, for not participating. Of course, those who are tactful, ambitious, or lonely participate in recreation that is not fun for them, but their later private remarks testify that it should have been. Similarly, children, mental patients, and prisoners may not have an effective option when officials declare game-time, but it is precisely in being thus constrained that these unfortunates seem something less than persons.

Because serious activity need not justify itself in terms of the fun it provides, we have neglected to develop an analytical view of fun and an appreciation of the light that fun throws on interaction in general. This paper attempts to see how far one can go by treating fun seriously. It begins as if addressing itself to a general consideration of social interaction, drawing on games for some illustrations. Only later will the question of fun in games be raised, and only at the end will any kind of answer be attempted.

2. *Encounters*. I limit myself to one type of social arrangement that occurs when persons are in one another's immediate physical presence, to be called here an *encounter* or a *focused gathering*. For the participants, this involves: a single visual and cognitive focus of attention; a mutual and preferential openness to verbal communication; a heightened mutual relevance of acts; an eye-to-eye ecological huddle that maximizes each participant's opportunity to perceive

2. Roger Caillois, in his very useful paper, 'Unity of Play: Diversity of Games', *Diogenes*, no. 19 (1957), p. 99. See also Johan Huizinga, *Homo Ludens* (Boston: Beacon Press, 1950), p. 28.

the other participants' monitoring of him.[3] Given these communication arrangements, their presence tends to be acknowledged or ratified through expressive signs, and a 'we rationale' is likely to emerge, that is, a sense of the single thing that *we* are doing together at the time. Ceremonies of entrance and departure are also likely to be employed, as are signs acknowledging the initiation and termination of the encounter or focused gathering as a unit. Whether bracketed by ritual or not, encounters provide the communication base for a circular flow of feeling among the participants as well as corrective compensations for deviant acts.

Examples of focused gatherings are: a *tête-à-tête*; a jury deliberation; a game of cards; a couple dancing; a task jointly pursued by persons physically close to one another; love-making; boxing. Obviously, taking turns at talking is not the only kind of activity upon which focused gatherings are built. Where a jointly sustained physical task is featured, the terms 'encounter' and 'focused gathering' may seem inappropriate, and a more abstract term, such as 'situated activity system', may be used. It should also be added: that persons present to each other need not be engaged in any encounter, constituting, therefore, an 'unfocused gathering'; that persons immediately present to each other can be parceled out into different encounters, as all partygoers know – a 'multi-focused gathering'; and that persons ostensibly engaged in one encounter can simultaneously sustain an additional 'subordinated' one. In the last instance the 'subordinated' encounter is sustained through covert expressions or by deferential restriction of the second encounter so that it does not get in the way of the officially dominating one.

FORMALIZATIONS

1. *Rules of Irrelevance*. Encounters are everywhere, but it is difficult to describe sociologically the stuff that they are made of. I fall back on the assumption that, like any other element of social life, an encounter exhibits sanctioned orderliness arising from obligations ful-

---

3. The term 'encounter' has a range of everyday meaning that reduces its value as a general term. Sometimes it is used to refer to face-to-face meetings with another that were unexpected or in which trouble occurred; sometimes it refers to meeting another at a social occasion, the frequency of comings-together during the occasion not being the issue. All these meanings I have to exclude.

filled and expectations realized, and that therein lies its structure. Presumably, we could learn about the structure of focused gatherings by examining what happens when their orderliness breaks down. Another method recommends itself, however. It seems characteristic of encounters, as distinguished from other elements of social organization, that their order pertains largely to what shall be attended and disattended, and through this, to what shall be accepted as the definition of the situation. (Of course, *what* definition of the situation the encounter will be obliged to maintain is often determined by the social occasion or affair in whose domain the encounter takes place.) Instead of beginning by asking what happens when this definition of the situation breaks down, we can begin by asking what perspectives this definition of the situation excludes when it is being satisfactorily sustained.[4]

Here, games can serve as a starting point. They clearly illustrate how participants are willing to forswear for the duration of the play any apparent interest in the esthetic, sentimental, or monetary value of the equipment employed, adhering to what might be called *rules of irrelevance*. For example, it appears that whether checkers are played with bottle tops on a piece of squared linoleum, with gold figurines on inlaid marble, or with uniformed men standing on colored flagstones in a specially arranged court square, the pairs of players can start with the 'same' positions, employ the same sequence of strategic moves and countermoves, and generate the same contour of excitement.

The elegance and strength of this structure of inattention to most things of the world is a great tribute to the social organization of human propensities. Witness the fugue-like manner in which deeply engrossed chess players are willing to help each other reposition a piece that has been brushed aside by a sleeve, dissociating this event from relevant reality and providing us with a clear example of a fundamental process, the sustaining of a subordinate side-encounter simultaneously with a main one that has been accorded the accent of reality. Another example of this is seen in 'wall games', wherein

4. I draw my orientation here from Harold Garfinkel, especially his 'Some Conceptions of and Experiments With "Trust" as a Condition of Stable Concerted Action', unpublished paper. A recent application of this paper may be found in A. K. Cohen, 'The Study of Social Disorganization and Deviant Behavior', in R. K. Merton, L. Broom and L. S. Cottrell, Jr, *Sociology Today* (New York: Basic Books, 1959), pp. 461–84, especially p. 474 ff.

school children, convicts, prisoners of war, or mental patients are ready to redefine an imprisoning wall as a part of the board that the game is played on, a board constituted of special rules of play, not bricks and mortar.[5] In Bateson's apt term, games place a 'frame' around a spate of immediate events, determining the type of 'sense' that will be accorded everything within the frame.[6] Rules of irrelevance are strictly applied, but, of course, only for the duration of the playing. At other times, the player will be fully alive to the game equipment as something to be cherished as an heirloom, given as an expensive gift, or stowed away in an unlocked drawer along with other cheap and easily replaceable possessions. These meanings are part of other frames in which game equipment can be handled; they cause confusion only when the individual 'breaks frame' and tries disrespectfully to assert one perspective when another was expected to hold sway.

Just as properties of the material context are held at bay and not allowed to penetrate the mutual activity of an encounter, so also certain properties of the participants will be treated as if they were not present. For this let us move from games to social parties. Simmel's famous description of the encounters of 'pure sociability' provides examples:

> The fact is that whatever the participants in the gathering may possess in terms of objective attributes – attributes that are centered outside the particular gathering in question – must not enter it. Wealth, social position, erudition, fame, exceptional capabilities and merits, may not play any part in sociability. At most they may perform the role of mere nuances of that immaterial character with which reality alone, in general, is allowed to enter the social work of art called sociability. [7]

> Sociability is the game in which one 'does as if' all were equal, and at the same time, as if one honored each of them in particular.[8]

This reduction of the personal character which homogenous interaction with others imposes on the individual may even make him lean over backward, if we may say so: a characteristically sociable behavior trait is the

5. See, for example, P. R. Reid, *Escape from Colditz* (New York: Berkley Publishing Corp., 1952), p. 63.

6. Gregory Bateson, 'A Theory of Play and Fantasy', *Psychiatric Research Reports 2* (American Psychiatric Association, 1955), p. 44.

7. Georg Simmel, *The Sociology of Georg Simmel*, trans. K. H. Wolff (Glencoe: The Free Press, 1950), pp. 45–6.

8. ibid., p. 49.

courtesy with which the strong and extraordinary individual not only makes himself the equal of the weaker, but even acts as if the weaker were the more valuable and superior.[9]

Simmel's embarrassing effort to treat sociability as a type of 'mere' play, sharply cut off from the entanglements of serious life, may be partly responsible for sociologists having failed to identify the rules of irrelevance in sociability with similar rules in serious areas of life. A good example of these rules in the latter areas is found in the impersonal calculable aspects of Western bureaucratic administration. Here, Weber supplies an obvious text, providing only that, as in the case of Simmel, we accept as a tendency what is stated as a fact:

> The 'objective' discharge of business primarily means a discharge of business according to *calculable rules* and 'without regard for persons'.
> 'Without regard for persons' is also the watchword of the 'market' and, in general, of all pursuits of naked economic interests. A consistent execution of bureaucratic domination means the leveling of status 'honor...'
> The second element mentioned, 'calculable rules', also is of paramount importance for modern bureaucracy. The peculiarity of modern culture, and specifically of its technical and economic basis, demands this very 'calculability' of results. When fully developed, bureaucracy also stands, in a specific sense, under the principle of *sine ira ac studio*. Its specific nature, which is welcomed by capitalism, develops the more perfectly the more the bureaucracy is 'dehumanized', the more completely it succeeds in eliminating from official business love, hatred, and all purely personal, irrational, and emotional elements which escape calculation.[10]

> ... the characteristic principle of bureaucracy [is] the abstract regularity of the execution of authority, which is a result of the demand for 'equality before the law' in the personal and functional sense – hence, of the horror of 'privilege', and the principled rejection of doing business 'from case to case'.[11]

While the explicit content of these statements is directed to administrative organization, not to focused gatherings, we must appreciate that a crucial part of the conduct of business, government, and the law has to do with the way in which an official handles clients or customers in direct face-to-face dealings. Parsons's reworking of Weber

9. ibid., pp. 48–9.
10. Max Weber, *From Max Weber: Essays in Sociology*, trans. and ed. H. H. Gerth and C. W. Mills (New York: Oxford University Press, 1946), pp. 215–16. The stress appears in the original.
11. ibid., p. 224.

presents this aspect of bureaucracy more clearly, especially in the concepts of 'universalism' and 'affective neutrality' as illustrated in professional–client relationships in medicine:

Affective neutrality is also involved in the physician's role as an applied scientist. The physician is expected to treat an objective problem in objective, scientifically justifiable terms. For example whether he likes or dislikes the particular patient as a person is supposed to be irrelevant, as indeed it is to most purely objective problems of how to handle a particular disease.[12]

In his initial work, Parsons was primarily concerned with distinctive features of the high professions, but, interestingly, any well-established business in Western society would have done almost as well. Salespersons in large, well-known stores have an ethic leading them to treat all customers with equal courtesy, whatever the customer's status or the probable value of his purchase. The phrase 'courteous service' points to the common expectation that an employee will show invariable good humor and consideration regardless of obvious social differences among customers.

Just as we find that certain social attributes are excluded from significance in wide ranges of encounters, so also we find that participants will hold in check certain psychological states and attitudes, for, after all, the very general rule that one enter into the prevailing mood in the encounter carries the understanding that contradictory feelings will be held in abeyance. Simmel states this theme in his discussion of the management of affect during social parties:

It is tactless, because it militates against *inter*action which monopolizes sociability, to display merely personal moods of depression, excitement, despondency – in brief, the light and the darkness of one's most intimate life.[13]

So generally in fact, does one suppress unsuitable affect, that we need to look at offenses to this rule to be reminded of its usual operation. Here, of course, Freud's ideas are central, for whether Freud deals

12. Talcott Parsons, *The Social System* (Glencoe: The Free Press, 1951), p. 435. For an additional treatment of universalism and affective neutrality, see the essay in which Parsons first employed the terms extensively, 'The Professions and Social Structure', reprinted as ch. 8, pp. 185–99, in his *Essays in Sociological Theory Pure and Applied* (Glencoe: The Free Press, 1949). A formal definition of 'universalism' may also be found in T. Parsons and E. Shils, ed., *Toward a General Theory of Action* (Cambridge: Harvard University Press, 1952), p. 82.

13. Simmel, op. cit., p. 46.

with 'faulty, chance, and symptomatic actions', or dreams, or wit of the 'overdetermined' kind, or serious manifestations of neurosis, he deals with the kinds of feelings that the offender's fellow-participants in the encounter are suppressing. Freud deals directly with the whole range of feelings, thoughts, and attitudes that fail to be successfully held back and hence, only less directly, with rules regarding what is allowed expression:

... the peculiar mode of operation, whose most striking function we recognize in the dream content, should not be attributed only to the sleeping state of the psychic life, when we possess abundant proof of its activity during the waking state in faulty actions. The same connection also forbids us from assuming that these psychic processes which impress us as abnormal and strange, are determined by deep-seated decay of psychic activity or by morbid state of function.

The correct understanding of this strange psychic work, which allows the faulty actions to originate like the dream pictures, will only be possible after we have discovered that the psychoneurotic symptoms, particularly the psychic formations of hysteria and compulsion neurosis, repeat in their mechanisms all the essential features of this mode of operation. The continuation of our investigation would therefore have to begin at this point.

But the common character of the mildest, as well as the severest cases, to which the faulty and chance actions contribute, *lies in the ability to refer the phenomena to unwelcome, repressed, psychic material, which, though pushed away from consciousness, is nevertheless not robbed of all capacity to express itself.*[14]

Cruder instances can be found in any mental hospital during those moments when the patient behaves in such a way as to make the psychiatrist feel that affect 'inappropriate in the situation' is being shown (as when, for example, a patient at mealtime asks for the salt in a voice that covers the whole table with misery and gloom), for what will later be seen as a 'symptom' first comes to attention because it is an infraction of a rule regarding affect restraint during daily encounters.

An interesting aspect of this affective discipline has to do with the amount of open self-reference a participant employs during informal conversational encounters. In fact, socialization in our society can be measured by the rate at which a child foregoes frank demands to

14. Sigmund Freud, *The Basic Writings of Sigmund Freud* (New York: Modern Library, 1938), pp. 177–8. The passage occurs as the ending to his monograph, *Psychopathology of Everyday Life*; the stress is in the original.

'look at me' or 'watch me do this',[15] just as 'desocialization' is felt
to be measurable by an increasing openness and persistence of self-
reference.

Just as certain desires and feelings are held in abeyance for the
duration of the encounter, so also we often find that the participant
disengages himself from undertakings that cut across the duration
and personnel of the current encounter. Patent involvement in what
has happened before the encounter or what is scheduled to occur after
it can be seen as preoccupation, restlessness, or impatience; and
unless special legitimating circumstances are present, disrespect for
the others present and undesirable qualities of personality are conveyed.

I have suggested that the character of an encounter is based in part
upon rulings as to properties of the situation that should be considered irrelevant, out of frame, or not happening. To adhere to these
rules is to play fair. Irrelevant visible events will be disattended;
irrelevant private concerns will be kept out of mind. An effortless unawareness will be involved, and if this is not possible then an active
turning-away or suppression will occur. Heroic examples of this quite
fundamental process – the operation of rules of irrelevance in social
interaction – can be discovered in mental hospitals, where patients
can be found immersed in a game of bridge (or affecting this immer-
sion) while one or two of the players engage in occult manneristic
movements and the whole table is surrounded by the clamor of
manic patients. Here it can be clearly seen that an engaging activity
acts as a boundary around the participants, sealing them off from
many potential worlds of meaning and action. Without this en-
circling barricade, presumably, participants would be immobilized
by an inundation of bases of action.

2. *Realized Resources.* The social organization exhibited in a focused
gathering is, then, a consequence of the effective operation of rules
of irrelevance. But, although this describes what is excluded from
the reality of the encounter, it tells us nothing about what is included,
and it is of this that we must now try to get a systematic view.

Again, games can provide a beginning. The set of rules which tells
us what should not be given relevance tells us also what we are to
treat as real. There can be an event only because a game is in progress,

15. In Catholic nunneries, apparently, this training is elaborated in a remarkable discipline that forbids all possible 'singularization', all ways of putting oneself forward or apart from the rest.

generating the possibility of an array of game-meaningful happenings. A 'schema of expression and interpretation' is involved:

> To illustrate, bridge players do not respond to each other's actions as behavioral events. They do not treat the fact that the other player withdraws a card from his hand and places it on the table as the event 'putting down a pasteboard' or 'effecting a translation of position of a card', but rather through the translation of the card's position the players signalizes that 'he has played the ace of spades as the first card of the trick'. From the player's point of view the question 'What can happen?' is for him correctly decided in terms of these rules.[16]

In addition to these game-meaningful events, we find game-generated roles or identities. When a capture occurs in chess, something happens relative to the lore and culture of the game, not merely to the board positions, for a piece of given power and status is the captor and another with a character of its own is the captive. It is only in baseball that the event 'grounding out to third' can occur. It is also only in baseball, however, that we can find the position of third baseman, along with the range of difficult situations this player is likely to have to face and the qualities of mind and body he will need to meet these situations well.

A matrix of possible events and a cast of roles through whose enactment the events occur constitute together a field for fateful dramatic action, a plane of being, an engine of meaning, a world in itself, different from all other worlds except the ones generated when the same game is played at other times. Riezler provides a statement of this theme in his fine paper on play and seriousness:

> I begin with the most simple case. We play games such as chess or bridge. They have rules the players agree to observe. These rules are not the rules of the 'real' world or of 'ordinary' life. Chess has its king and queen, knights and pawns, its space, its geometry, its laws of motion, its demands, and its goal. The queen is not a real queen, nor is she a piece of wood or ivory. She is an entity in the game defined by the movements the game allows her. The game is the context within which the queen is what she is. This context is not the context of the real world or of ordinary life. The game is a little cosmos of its own.[17]

Games, then, are world-building activities. I want to suggest that serious activities have this quality too. We are ready to see that there

16. Garfinkel, op. cit., p. 7.

17. Kurt Riezler, 'Play and Seriousness', *The Journal of Philosophy*, 38 (1941), pp. 505–17.

is no world outside the various playings of a game that quite corresponds to the game-generated reality, but we have been less willing to see that the various instances of a serious encounter generate a world of meanings that is exclusive to it. It is only around a small table that one can show coolness in poker or the capacity to be bluffed out of a pair of aces; but, similarly, it is only on the road that the roles of motorist and pedestrian take on full meaning, and it is only among persons avowedly joined in a state of talk that we can learn something of the meaning of half-concealed inattentiveness or relative frequency of times each individual talks. (Of course, the equipment employed in some serious encounters is not as well adapted for cosmos building as are game materials, for wider reality is rarely as well designed to be psychologically real as is a game designed just for this purpose; full-fledged identities may not emerge and, as will be considered later, a full mutual fatefulness may not arise from the moves taken by the players.)

How can we characterize these worlds of face-to-face interaction? We cannot say they belong to fantasy, at least not if we are going to argue that serious, as well as unserious, encounters generate these involvements. We cannot say the worlds are created on the spot, because, whether we refer to a game of cards or to teamwork during surgery, use is usually made of traditional equipment having a social history of its own in the wider society and a wide consensus of understanding regarding the meanings that are to be generated from it. It is only in certain interactional settings that there can arise what is said through a loving kiss; but to generate this type of event is not to invent it. Nor can we say that the encounter world includes everything that happens on the spot. In every encounter, for example, there will be locally generated sounds and locally performed body movements that are disattended, whether automatically or studiously, being barred from reality by rules of irrrelevance. We can, however, say this about the worlds of focused gatherings: the material for realizing the full range of events and roles of these worlds is locally available to the participants.

I propose to try to analyse focused gatherings on the assumption that each can be viewed as having carved everything needed from the stuffs at hand; the elements of each encounter will be treated as if they consituted a full deck. There is no combination of bids and hands that any deck of cards might not bring to any table of bridge, providing the players sit long enough; in the same way, a customer, a clerk, and a floor manager can among themselves play out the drama that is possible in shops. I shall refer to these locally realizable events and roles as *realized resources*.[18]

Just as every encounter will sustain events that are part of a world that can be fully realized within the encounter, so many of the matters that are given no concern or attention will have an organizational base and a relevant world of meaning beyond the confines of the type of encounter in question. When the boss comes to dinner and is treated 'the same as any other guest', the matter that is shown no consideration, whether automatically or carefully, is one that requires us to move from the employee's house to the business establishment for its full realization. When a man does not give way to preoccupation with his child ill at home but participates fully in the spirit of a golf game with his cronies, it is again an externally grounded matter that is being kept from the field of attention. Such externally grounded matters, not realized within the engagement, have a continuing significance outside the current encounter and outside encounters of that type.

3. *Transformation Rules*. Given the presence of realized resources, it is apparent that in each focused gathering the problem of how to allocate these resources among the participants must be solved.[19] Whatever the various solutions, it is apparent that attributes of participants will have to be employed as means for deciding on allocation. Some of these allocative attributes can be fully generated by means of a special preliminary encounter, as when bridge partners are selected according to a little game of highs and lows in a draw of cards, or when numbered cards are given out in a bakery shop to mark priority of appearance. In other cases the allocative attributes may derive directly from the realized world of the encounter, as when prizes are distributed according to game score.

Now it is possible to imagine a focused gathering where almost all externally based matters (including externally based attributes of participants) are treated as officially irrelevant. Thus, a game of checkers played between two strangers in a hospital admissions ward

18. R. F. Bales, *Interaction Process Analysis* (Cambridge: Addison-Wesley, 1950), pp. 73–84, employs the term 'resources', but defines it as merely one item for distribution, the others being authority, honor, and group solidarity.

19. Interest in allocative processes has recently been stimulated by the work of Talcott Parsons, especially T. Parsons and N. J. Smelser, *Economy and Society* (Glencoe: The Free Press, 1956), pp. 51–100.

may constitute orderly interaction that is officially independent of
sex, age, language, socio-economic status, physical and mental condition, religion, staff-patient hierarchy, and so forth. But, in actual fact,
externally realized matters are given some official place and weight in
most encounters, figuring as avowed elements in the situation, even if
only as determinants of the terms of address employed, as when two
customers are treated alike except that one is called Sir and the other
Miss. In the classic phrase of England's gentry, 'Anyone for tennis?'
did not quite mean *anyone*; it is not recorded that a servant has ever
been allowed to define himself as an *anyone*, although such doubtful
types as tutors have occasionally been permitted to do so.[20] The role
of chairman of the meeting is a locally realized resource, but the discussion may deal with matters that are not wholly at hand, just as the
question of who fills the chair may be settled by externally based factors, such as stock ownership. The solid barrier by which participants
in an encounter cut themselves off from externally based matters now
seems to be not quite solid; like a sieve, it allows a few externally
based matters to seep through into the encounter.

These externally realized but officially accredited matters seem
more frequently to decide who is allowed or required to participate
in the encounter than how resources are distributed once the participants have been selected, but the latter is possible. Thus, in sociable
bridge games, which could well be arranged by drawing for partner
and deal, husband and wife often are required either to play opposite
each other, or not to, in either case introducing in a formal way the
matter of marriage. The issue here, however, is that an externally
realized property that is given official relevance as an allocative attri-

20. It should be noted that two types of exclusion can be involved here, one
determining who will participate with whom in a given type of encounter, and a
second, less obvious, determining who will be allowed to participate in this type
of encounter under any circumstances. In the sociologist's Golden Age of England, servants would have been considered above themselves to play tennis even
amongst themselves. Similarly, there have been times when chess was restricted
to court circles, and there are records of punishment given to those who boot-
legged the game. (For this and other aspects of the 'royal game', see the interesting paper by Norman Reider, 'Chess, Oedipus and the Mater Dolorosa', *The
International Journal of Psycho-Analysis*, 40 (1959), reprinted in *Psychoanalysis
and the Psychoanalytic Review*, 47 (1960).) In our own society we have an array of
state laws specifying that females below a given age cannot participate in sexual
encounters with anyone and that females above this age can participate only with
certain categories of others.

bute still functions as a way of excluding *other* such attributes.[21] A clear example is a state dinner, where precedence at table is given according to governmental rank; for this externally based attribute to function locally, ranks of nobility have to be specifically excluded as a determinant of precedence, and quite explicitly are.[22]

We have now arrived at the following formulation of the order sustained in an encounter: a locally realized world of roles and events cuts the participants off from many externally based matters that might have been given relevance, but allows a few of these external matters to enter the interaction world as an official part of it. Of special importance are those properties in the wider world that constitute attributes of the encounter's participants, for these attributes are potential determinants of the way in which locally realized resources are distributed.

We must next go on to see that it is not simply a question of some potentially determinative attributes being allowed an allocative function and others not. Little understanding of the realm of social interaction can be obtained unless we recognize that in most cases the resources fully realized within an encounter cannot be allocated in a pattern that corresponds completely with the pattern in which the attribute is distributed in the wider world. We are in the habit of speaking of certain externally based attributes as being 'expressed' within the mutual activity of a focused gathering, as when the boss is given the seat of honor at dinner or the eldest person present is allowed to determine when work will begin or end. With certain exceptions, however, the means of giving expression to these external matters are not refined enough to express all the externally based nuances. Thus, the locally generated and realized honor shown a boss at table may have to be used on another occasion for a visitor from out of town, a family member back from the hospital, a child recently graduated from primary to secondary school, or our first-mentioned boss's boss. And the seat of second honor at table may go to the second-ranking person, regardless of how close or distant his social position is to that of the guest of honor. The seat of honor

21. Often, of course, by employing externally based attributes that are either taken for granted or trivial (such as length of diplomatic residence), other externally based attributes that might be in dispute can be excluded from the situation.

22. Emily Post, *Etiquette* (New York: Funk and Wagnalls, 1937), p. 681. Rank is always official. This means that plain Mr Smith, who has become 'His Excellency the Ambassador', ranks a Prince or a Duke who is officially a Secretary of Embassy.

can show precedence only, and this ordering is only a rough reflection of the infinitely different sets of relationships that can exist among those present by virtue of their socio-economic and membership characteristics. In general, then, the 'regard' or 'respect' that events in an encounter can be made to show for the externally based attributes of participants can be only a gesture in the right direction, accurately 'expressing' only a very abstract aspect of structures in the wider world.

The question of what happens to an externally based attribute when it passes through the boundary of an encounter is even more complicated, however: it is possible not only to block (or randomize) externally based properties, or to allow them some rough expression, but also to introduce them in a partially reversed way – the negative ordering illustrated in our Biblical belief that 'the last shall be first and the first last'. Thus, many of the minor courtesies that men display to children or women in our society have this inverted character, with honor going to the youngest or weakest, not because youth and frailness are honored, but as a ceremonial reversal of ordinary practice. More extreme instances of this can be found during certain ceremonials and festivities. As Gluckman suggests:

> In certain armed services at Christmas, and at Christmas only, the officers wait at table on the men. This kind of reversal of rôle is well known in ceremonial and ritual.[23]

> Similarly, in the Polish ghettos, where the rabbis were powerful, once a year a sermon attacking them was preached in the synagogue by a wastrel . . .[24]

An institutional version of this can be found in many 'total institutions', where annual skits and plays are produced in which students play the roles of professors, patients, the roles of psychiatrists, a prisoner the role of warden.[25] So, too, when a West Indian voodoo performance occurs, those who feel driven to come forward and play a leading role may be those to whom the community at large has accorded a low position.[26]

23. Max Gluckman, *Custom and Conflict in Africa* (Glencoe: The Free Press, 1955), p. 109.

24. ibid., p. 132.

25. E. Goffman, 'The Characteristics of Total Institutions', in *Symposium on Preventive and Social Psychiatry* (Washington, D.C.: Walter Reed Army Institute of Research, April 15–17, 1957), pp. 77–8.

26. Alfred Métraux, 'Dramatic Elements in Ritual Possession', *Diogenes*, no. 11 (1955), p. 29.

Let us now take stock once again. We have been focusing our attention on the boundary between the wider world and the mutual activity embedded in a focused gathering, and we have asked how properties from the outside world are selectively handled within the encounter. We found that the barrier to externally realized properties was more like a screen than like a solid wall, and we then came to see that the screen not only selects but also transforms and modifies what is passed through it. Speaking more strictly, we can think of inhibitory rules that tell participants what they must not attend to and of facilitating rules that tell them what they may recognize. (Together these rules represent one of the great themes of social organization, being one basic way in which every encounter is embedded in society.) We find, then, *transformation rules*, in the geometrical sense of that term, these being rules, both inhibitory and facilitating, that tell us what modification in shape will occur when an external pattern of properties is given expression inside the encounter.

The transformation rules of an encounter describe the fate of any property as a constituent of internal order. I have given special attention to externally based social attributes because these are of central interest in traditional sociological analysis. A consideration of these attributes in relation to the transformation rules of encounters allows us to deal directly and analytically with face-to-face instances of what are ordinarily called 'deference patterns', defining deference here as interpersonal ritual.[27] These patterns establish the manner in which social attributes crucial in the wider society are dealt with during concrete occasions of face-to-face interaction.

DYNAMICS OF ENCOUNTERS

1. *Games, Play, and Gaming.* Until now in this paper, it has been useful to draw informally on games for illustrations of face-to-face

27. See E. Goffman, 'The Nature of Deference and Demeanor', *American Anthropologist*, 58 (1956), pp. 473–502. Recent interest in comparing the character of large-scale societies, partly deriving from a re-reading of travel accounts, such as that of de Tocqueville, has led to describing the character of a society by the equalitarian or inequalitarian character of the personal encounters occurring in it, especially those occurring in public and semi-public places. While the transformation rules for public conduct are an important element of a society, they certainly do not provide us with a description of its social structure. There is a large difference between the distribution of substantive rights and power in a society and the distribution of conversational courtesies.

interaction. There certainly are precedents for this. Students of social activity are increasingly using traditional and experimental games as working models. Games seem to display in a simple way the structure of real-life situations. They cut us off from serious life by immersing us in a demonstration of its possibilities. We return to the world as gamesmen, prepared to see what is structural about reality and ready to reduce life to its liveliest elements.

A game-theoretical approach also involves, however, important limitations in the study of face-to-face interaction. Before these limitations can be perceived and dealt with, we must look more carefully at the perspective from which they derive, introducing such definitions as seem necessary.

The game model has very serious implications for the accepted language of social psychology, especially for three key concepts, the individual, communication, and interaction.[28] The concept of the 'individual' is properly split in two. We now have an 'interest-identity', 'team', or 'side', this being something without flesh or blood that profits or loses by the outcome of the game according to a known utility function; and we have a 'player', an agent-of-play, not a principal, who thinks and acts but does this for the side on which he is playing. The concept of 'communicative activity' is similarly altered: the basic activity in a game is a *move*, and moves are neither communicated like messages nor performed like tasks and deeds; they are *made* or *taken*. To make a move requires some social arrangement by which a principal, acting through his agent, can commit himself to a position. To communicate that this position has been taken up is another move, quite distinct from the first, as is demonstrated by the fact that often in games our object is to make a move without informing the opposing team that we have made it. Finally, as regards interaction, we see that a game perspective reduces the situation to teams, each acting rationally to press a single type of interest or pay-off while accepting very special conditions of action. Each move must be selected from a small number of possibilities, these being largely determined by the previous move of the opposing team, just as each move largely determines the possibilities next open to the opponent. Each team is aware of this mutual determination and oriented to the control of it, the entire outcome for each team being dependent on how it fares in this out-

28. Here I draw on the work of T. C. Schelling, now available in his *The Strategy of Conflict* (Cambridge: Harvard University Press, 1960).

maneuvering. The concept of interaction is thus transformed: instead of referring to mutual influence that might be peripheral and trivial, it now refers to a highly structured form of mutual fatefulness.

In the literature on games, a distinction is made between a *game*, defined as a body of rules associated with a lore regarding good strategies, and a *play*, defined as any particular instance of a given game being played from beginning to end.[29] *Playing* could then be defined as the process of move-taking through which a given play is initiated and eventually completed; action is involved, but only the strictly game-relevant aspects of action.

There are games, such as poker and bridge, which seem to require the players to sit facing each other around a small table. There are other games, such as hide-and-go-seek and war exercises, which fix the playing organically to a time and space but nevertheless require opposing teams to be out of each other's sight. There are still other games, such as chess, that ordinarily bring the players together but sometimes are played through the mails by enthusiasts without restriction to a time and space.

The varieties of interaction that occur among persons who are face to face for the avowed purpose of carrying on a game, I shall call *gaming*, including here, in addition to playing, activity that is not strictly relevant to the outcome of the play and cannot be defined in terms of the game. I shall call a focused gathering that ostensibly features plays of a game a *gaming encounter*. A play of a game has players; a gaming encounter has participants.[30] A play is a special abstraction from the more concrete unit, gaming encounter, just as the concept of player is an abstraction from that of participant.

By this time, it can be seen that a gaming encounter will be differently analyzed depending on whether it is seen as the occasion for plays of a game or as the occasion of gaming. The first kind of subject matter is codifiable and clean, the second is very sticky. Between the time when four persons sit down to bridge and the time when all four leave the table, an organic system of interaction has come into being. Whether there occur many plays of the game or an incomplete single

29. John von Neumann and Oskar Morgenstern, *Theory of Games and Economic Behavior* (Princeton University Press, 1944), p. 49.

30. Compare here the helpful discussion of the difference between official game and spectacle in K. L. Pike, *Language in Relation to a Unified Theory of the Structure of Human Behavior* (Glendale, Calif.: Summer Institute of Linguistics, 1954), Part I, pp. 44–5.

play may be of secondary importance, marking only slight shifts and turns in the contour of feeling. (An incomplete play can provide the joint activity of a fairly well-terminated encounter.) When one player takes time out to answer the telephone, the play may be stopped in mid-air, being transfixable for any period of time, but not the social affair, the gaming encounter, for this can be threatened and even destroyed if the absent player is held too long on the telephone or must return with tragic news. Similarly, players may tacitly agree to begin to toy with the play or to shift their interest away from it, yet this very threat to play may come from a strengthening of the participants' engrossment in the side-encounter that is a standard part of some gaming encounters. Further, although kibitzers may be officially tolerated on the assumption that they will conduct themselves so as to have no real effect upon the outcome of the play, they are likely to be an integral part of the social-psychological reality of the gaming encounter; they are participants, not players, and can have a leading role in the gaming encounter while having no role in the play. In any case we must note that while it is as players that we can win a play, it is only as participants that we can get fun out of this winning.

2. *Spontaneous Involvement.* What I have said about interaction in the section on formalizations holds for focused gatherings, including the chief example used, gaming encounters, but what was said there also holds for activity systems that are not realized within the boundaries of a face-to-face setting. For example, games played at a distance involve rules of irrelevance, a schema of interpretation, and resources realized fully within the possibilities of the game. Multi-situated game-like activities, such as the 'newspaper game' or the 'banking game',[31] which involve an occupational community, with motives and positions generated and realizable within the community, can also be analyzed in these terms. This breadth of application of what has so far been considered about encounters is underlined in codes of conduct, such as government protocol, which provide a

---

31. See, for example, Norton Long, 'The Local Community as an Ecology of Games', *American Journal of Sociology*, 64 (1958), pp. 251–6, especially p. 253. Kurt Riezler in *Man Mutable and Immutable* (Chicago: Regnery, 1950), p. 64, provides a succinct statement: 'When we speak of the world of the theatre, of politics, of journalism or high finance, we indicate a kind of unity of a way of thinking and living in a universe of response in which man aims at reputation, status, a weighty voice.'

single body of formalized rules for dealing with face-to-face encounters and negotiation at a distance.

Focused gatherings do, however, have unique and significant properties which a formalistic game-theoretical view of interaction tends to overlook. The most crucial of these properties, it seems to me, is the organismic psychobiological nature of spontaneous involvement.[32] To give proper weight to this component of face-to-face behavior, some psychological imputations are necessary.

When an individual becomes engaged in an activity, whether shared or not, it is possible for him to become caught up by it, carried away by it, engrossed in it – to be, as we say, spontaneously involved in it. He finds it psychologically unnecessary to refrain from dwelling on it and psychologically unnecessary to dwell on anything else. A visual and cognitive engrossment occurs, with an honest unawareness of matters other than the activity;[33] what Harry Stack Sullivan called 'selective inattention' occurs, with an effortless dissociation from all other events, distinguishing this type of unawareness both from suppression and repression.[34] When an individual engages in an encounter, his conscious awareness can bring certain shared things to life and deaden all other matters. By this spontaneous involvement in the joint activity, the individual becomes an integral part of the situation, lodged in it and exposed to it, infusing himself into the encounter in a manner quite different from the way an ideally rational player commits his side to a position in an ideally abstract game. As already considered, a game move is one thing; self-mobilization through which this move is executed during a gaming encounter is quite another. Game rules govern the one, the structure of gaming encounters governs the others.[35] I want to note here that while a

32. Among social psychologists, an explicit consideration of this element is given by T. R. Sarbin in 'Role Theory', section 'Organismic Dimension', pp. 233–5 in Gardner Lindzey, ed., *Handbook of Social Psychology* (Cambridge: Addison-Wesley, 1954). See also E. F. Borgatta and L. S. Cottrell, Jr, 'On the Classification of Groups', *Sociometry*, 18 (1955), pp. 416–18.

33. E. Goffman, 'Alienation from Interaction', *Human Relations*, 10 (1957), p. 47.

34. H. S. Sullivan, *Clinical Studies in Psychiatry* (New York: Norton, 1956), pp. 38–76, especially pp. 63–4.

35. This is not to say that formally relevant strategies for playing games will not be required to take the world of concrete face-to-face interaction into consideration. Assessing a possible bluff is a formal part of the game of poker, the player being advised to examine his opponent's minor and presumably uncalculated expressive behavior. Games vary greatly in the use the player is obliged to

player's current position on a board often can be adequately conveyed by brief signals through the mails, evidence of his spontaneous involvement in the gaming encounter can be adequately conveyed only to those in his immediate presence.

Gaming encounters provide us with fine examples of how a mutual activity can utterly engross its participants, transforming them into worthy antagonists in spite of the triviality of the game, great differences in social status, and the patent claims of other realities. Of this, the daughter of a British Edwardian beauty reminds us in her autobiography:

> Sometimes, King Edward (Kingy) came to tea with Mamma, and was there when I appeared at six o'clock. On such occasions he and I devised a fascinating game. With a fine disregard for the good condition of his trouser, he would lend me his leg, on which I used to start two bits of bread and butter (butter side down), side by side. Then, bets of a penny each were made (my bet provided by Mamma) and the winning piece of bread and butter depended, of course, on which was the more buttery. The excitement was intense while the contest was on. Sometimes he won, sometimes I did. Although the owner of a Derby winner, Kingy's enthusiasm seemed delightfully unaffected by the quality of his bets.[36]

And even when a gaming encounter begins with self-consciousness and reserve on the part of the players, we often find that the ice is soon broken and all players are being called by a familiar term of address.

It is not only possible for participants to become involved in the encounter in progress, but it is also defined as obligatory that they sustain this involvement in given measure; too much is one kind of delict; too little, another. There is no equivalent to this crucial interaction obligation in the formal logic of games, but here is a basic similarity between gaming encounters and other types of focused gatherings: both can be taken too seriously, both not seriously enough.

Why should the factor of spontaneous involvement carry so much

---

make of apparently non-game aspects of the local concrete situation; in checkers, little attention need be given to such matters, in poker, much. Further, formal rules in some games are expressly concerned with the social-psychological character of gaming, so that, for example, when time out is permitted, a time limit to the rest period may be stipulated.

36. Sonia Keppel, *Edwardian Daughter* (New York: British Book Centre, 1959), pp. 22–3.

weight in the organization of encounters? Some suggestions can be made. A participant's spontaneous involvement in the official focus of attention of an encounter tells others what he is and what his intentions are, adding to the security of the others in his presence. Further, shared spontaneous involvement in a mutual activity often brings the sharers into some kind of exclusive solidarity and permits them to express relatedness, psychic closeness, and mutual respect; failure to participate with good heart can therefore express rejection of those present or of the setting. Finally, spontaneous involvement in the prescribed focus of attention confirms the reality of the world prescribed by the transformation rules and the unreality of other potential worlds – and it is upon these confirmations that the stability of immediate definitions of the situation depends.

Assessment of spontaneous co-involvement may be particularly important during encounters with only two participants, for here the success or failure of the interaction in engrossing the participants may be perceived by them as having diagnostic significance for their relationship. Here love-making provides us with some extremely useful data, for the engrossing power of such encounters can become a crucial test of the relationship, while local physical happenings are very likely to distract at least one of the partners.[37] And we know that the relation between two persons can become such that, on whatever occasion they meet, they must – like two ex-husbands of the same woman – suppress considerations that they are not capable of banishing from mind, and thus spoil all occasions of interaction with one another.

The question of spontaneous co-involvement goes, then, to the heart of things and helps us isolate the special characteristics of face-to-face interaction. Multi-situated games and game-like activities can define the situation for their participants and create a world for them. But this is a loose world for the individual, allowing for periods of lack of interest and for wide variation in attitude and feelings, even though such multi-situated games, when institutionalized, can provide a kind of reality market – a world available whenever the individual

37. An excellent example may be found in a short story by William Sansom, 'The Kiss', in his *Something Terrible, Something Lovely* (New York: Harcourt, Brace, n.d.), pp. 54 7. This kind of encounter, if formalized in game theoretical terms, would clearly have some distinctive un-game-like features: once started, time out cannot easily be declared, kibitzers are usually lethal, and substitutes ordinarily cannot be brought in.

decides to dip into it. The world of a multi-situated game can be lightly invested in, so that while the game defines the situation it does not bring the situation into lively existence. 'Mere games' cannot easily be played at a distance because the chance of involving the participants may be too small; it is only devotees who play chess through the mails, a devotee by definition being someone who can become caught up in a sportive reality when rain, prolonged play, or play at a distance kills the game for others.

Face-to-face games, on the other hand, bear differently on one's sense of reality. That activity is going on before one's eyes ensures that a mere definition of the situation is experienced as having the thickness of reality. That other persons are involved ensures that engrossment must be steadily sustained in spite of the flickering of one's actual interest. Further, there seems to be no agent more effective than another person in bringing a world for oneself alive or, by a glance, a gesture, or a remark, shriveling up the reality in which one is lodged. It is only in face-to-face encounters that almost anything (even the game of buttered toast on King Edward's trousers) can become the basis of a perspective and a definition of the situation; it is only here that a definition of the situation has a favored chance of taking on the vivid character of sensed reality.

3. *Ease and Tension*. We come now to a crucial consideration. The world made up of the objects of our spontaneous involvement and the world carved out by the encounter's transformation rules can be congruent, one coinciding perfectly with the other. In such circumstances, what the individual is obliged to attend to, and the way in which he is obliged to perceive what is around him, will coincide with what can and what does become real to him through the natural inclination of his spontaneous attention. Where this kind of agreement exists, I assume – as an empirical hypothesis – that the participants will feel *at ease* or natural, in short, that the interaction will be *euphoric* for them.

But it is conceivable that the participant's two possible worlds – the one in which he is obliged to dwell and the one his spontaneous involvement actually does or could bring alive to him – may not coincide, so that he finds himself spontaneously engrossed in matters declared irrelevant and unreal by the transformation rules. I make a second empirical assumption, that a person who finds himself in this conflict will feel uneasy, bored, or unnatural in the situation, experiencing this to the degree that he feels committed to maintaining the transformation rules. Under such circumstances, we can say that a *state of tension* or *dysphoria* exists for him in the encounter; he feels *uneasy*. Note that two main situations are possible for the uneasy participant: he can find himself strongly drawn to matters officially excluded (this being the case we will mainly consider); or he can find himself strongly repelled by the official focus of attention, as when issues are raised that he has suppressed, causing him to feel self-conscious, overinvolved, and acutely uncomfortable.

The perception that one participant is not spontaneously involved in the mutual activity can discredit the identity imputed to him as someone who is able and ready to immerse himself in an encounter and can weaken for the others their own involvement in the encounter and their own belief in the reality of the world it prescribes. A perceived deviation from the norm can thus have a 'multiplier' effect, infecting the whole encounter.[38] In the same way, a model of appropriate involvement can shift the effect in the other direction and make for ease throughout. We must therefore allot a special place to the kind of uneasiness that can be managed unobtrusively and non-contagiously and to the kind of poise that equips the individual to do so. It is on this margin between being out of touch with the encounter and showing it that drinkers, addicts, and the emotionally bereaved concentrate, being greatly concerned to conceal their dereliction from interaction duties.

Although ease tends to be defined by persons as the 'normal' state of affairs, in actuality it seems to be rarely achieved for any length of time in ordinary life. It is here, of course, that recreational games shine, for in gaming encounters euphoric interaction is relatively often achieved: gaming is often fun. Again we can claim, then, that to understand how games can be 'fun' and what fun is, is to learn something important about all encounters.

It should be clearly understood that I have been using the term 'tension' (and its opposite, lack of tension, or ease), in a restricted and special sense. A man losing money at poker and waiting with tenseness for the next card need not be in a state of tension as here defined. The gaming encounter, as a source of shared, obligatory, spontaneous involvement, can still be fun for him. The same man winning what are for him insignificant sums from players he considers too unskilled to be worth beating might have little tenseness in the occasion, although sticking out an evening of the game might be a matter of

38. Goffman, 'Alienation', pp. 53–4.

considerable tension for him. As used here, tension refers, I repeat, to a sensed discrepancy between the world that spontaneously becomes real to the individual, or the one he is able to accept as the current reality, and the one in which he is obliged to dwell. This concept of tension is crucial to my argument, for I will try to show that just as the coherence and persistence of a focused gathering depends on maintaining a boundary, so the integrity of this barrier seems to depend upon the management of tension.

Under certain circumstances, persons can be so engrossed in an encounter that it is practically impossible to distract their attention; in such cases they can hardly feel ill at ease. Since we have this capacity to become engrossed, how is it we do not more often use it to avoid dysphoria?

One answer, of course, is that participants often feel alienated from the context of the interaction or from their fellow participants, and exploit any untoward event as a means of feeling and expressing disaffection. Another answer has to do with identity. The organization of an encounter and the definition of the situation it provides turn upon the conceptions the participants have concerning the identity of the participants and the identity of the social occasion of which the encounter is seen as a part. These identities are the organizational hub of the encounter. Events which cause trouble do not merely add disruptive noise but often convey information that threatens to discredit or supplant the organizing identities of the interaction. Hence, such events, however small in themselves, can weaken the whole design of the encounter, leaving the participants bewildered about what next to do, or what next to try to be.[39] In any case, of all our capacities, the one for spontaneous involvement seems to be least subject to conscious control – for to be concerned about being spontaneously involved in some activity is necessarily to be spontaneously involved in the concern, not the activity.

I have suggested that in any encounter there is likely to be some tension or dysphoria, some discrepancy between obligatory involvements and spontaneous ones. None the less, for any given encounter, it is of analytical interest to imagine those circumstances which would maximize ease or euphoria, bringing actual involvements and obligatory ones into perfect congruence. These circumstances we may refer to as the encounter's *euphoria function*. It will be apparent that a

39. E. Goffman, 'Embarrassment and Social Organization', *American Journal of Sociology*, 62 (1956), p. 268.

maximum of euphoria can be achieved in theory in two different ways: one, by granting the character of the activity and going on from there to obtain the most suitable recruits (in terms of the maintenance of euphoria); and, the other, by granting the recruits and, given their social attributes, determining the most effective allocation of internally-generated resources. For example, given the fact that it is the boss who is the guest at dinner, we can imagine that special combination of equality and deference that would best carry off the occasion; and given any particular allocation of locally realized resources, we can search out that dinner guest whose externally based social properties will be exactly the ones to make the occasion come off successfully.

Of course, we are unlikely to be able to manage social affairs so as to realize the euphoria function of a particular encounter, but it is useful to have this as a structural ideal, the end of a continuum along which actual events can be placed. Those who make up invitation lists for small social gatherings and table arrangements for large ones do in fact have a euphoria function in mind (although typically there will be other conditions that they must attempt to satisfy also).

Interestingly enough, the issue of a *dysphoria function* is worth considering too, and not only because of the fantasy persons sometimes have of giving a party with a maximally unsuitable combination of guests. Thus, it is reported that in order to keep resistance and morale low, those in charge of Chinese prisoner-of-war camps shifted 'natural' leaders from one group to another, and gave officially sponsored positions of power to those prisoners whose externally based attributes might make them least eligible as far as their fellow prisoners were concerned.[40]

4. *Incidents*. Two key concepts, transformation rules and interaction tension, have now been introduced, and suggestions have been made concerning their relationship; for example, while it is characteristic of focused gatherings that a set of transformation rules can be adhered to through wide alterations in tension, any alteration in transformation rules is likely to lead to a marked increase or decrease in tension. Now, if we grant that tension and transformation rules are two members of the same family of terms, we must try to see what the other members look like.

During an encounter events may occur, whether intended or not,

40. See E. H. Schein, 'The Chinese Indoctrination Program for Prisoners of War', *Psychiatry*, 19 (1956), p. 153.

that suddenly increase the level of tension. Following everyday usage, I will refer to such events as *incidents*.

Perhaps the most common type of incident, one to which Freud gave much attention in his *Psychopathology of Everyday Life*,[41] consists of what we ordinarily call slips, boners, gaffes, or malapropisms, which unintentionally introduce information that places a sudden burden on the suppressive work being done in the encounter.

While slips are felt to be unintentional, the person who makes them is none the less held somewhat responsible. A parallel type of incident results from what might be called 'leaky words': a term or phrase is used that has an appropriate and innocent meaning but also a sound that suddenly increases the difficulty of holding back official irrelevancies. In a high-school classroom, for example, sexual issues and sexual statuses may be effectively suppressed until a word is introduced whose homonymous alternate is frankly sexual, thus momentarily inundating the interaction with distracting considerations.

Another common type of incident is what might be called a 'sign situation', namely, the unintended and undesired occurrence of a configuration of environmental events which all too aptly expresses a recognition of identities theretofore easefully disattended. For example, two persons can carry on a conversation with effective unconcern for their difference in occupational status until the unplanned-for necessity of having to pass single file through a doorway causes both participants to consider how to manage the problem of priority without giving offence. The very need to conceal this concern may constitute a painful distraction from the conversation at hand.

It may be noted here that it is the special fate of handicapped persons, such as the blind or the lame, to create contexts in which leaky words and sign situations are likely to occur. Encounters that adhere to the tactful and standard rule of 'not noticing' the defects[42] are likely to have a precarious easefulness, since almost any physical

41. Especially the section 'Mistakes in Speech', pp. 69–86. In this monograph, Freud is mainly concerned with the meaning of unexpected phrasings as an expression of the speaker's unconscious or merely suppressed wishes and concerns. Later, in his *Wit and Its Relation to the Unconscious*, he gives more weight to what is our prime concern here, the relation of the incident to the encounter in which it occurs.

42. The rules of irrelevance for encounters in public life, through which physical handicaps are often officially treated as if they did not exist, are neatly described by Nigel Dennis in his brilliant story, 'A Bicycle Built for Two', *Encounter*, 15 (1960), pp. 12–22, especially pp. 14–15.

movement can set the stage for a sign situation and many common phrases can similarly inundate the encounter with previously suppressed or spontaneously unattended matters. Persons with a social stigma of a racial or ethnic kind, and those with a moral stigma, such as ex-mental patients, ex-convicts, and homosexuals, also share this predicament. Such individuals must learn to deal with the unhappy property of being inimical to almost every encounter in which they find themselves. The central issue in such an individual's life situation is not that he is going to be discriminated against but that when he interacts with an ordinary member of the community both attempt to suppress matters that are embarrrassingly more fundamental than the ones being explicitly considered – and make this attempt even while both ready themselves for the possibility of a breakdown in tact. Cooley provides an accurate statement of the consequence of this interaction predicament, with special reference to the mentally ill:

The peculiar relations to other persons attending any marked personal deficiency or peculiarity are likely to aggravate, if not to produce, abnormal manifestations of self-feeling. Any such trait sufficiently noticeable to interrupt easy and familiar intercourse with others, and make people talk and think *about* a person or *to* him rather than *with* him, can hardly fail to have this effect. If he is naturally inclined to pride or irritability, these tendencies, which depend for correction upon the flow of sympathy, are likely to be increased. One who shows signs of mental aberration is, inevitably perhaps, but cruelly, shut off from familiar, thoughtless intercourse, partly excommunicated; his isolation is unwittingly proclaimed to him on every countenance by curiosity, indifference, aversion, or pity, and in so far as he is human enough to need free and equal communication and feel the lack of it, he suffers pain and loss of a kind and degree which others can only faintly imagine, and for the most part ignore. He finds himself apart, 'not in it', and feels chilled, fearful, and suspicious. Thus 'queerness' is no sooner perceived than it is multiplied by reflection from other minds. The same is true in some degree of dwarfs, deformed or disfigured persons, even the deaf and those suffering from the infirmities of old age.[43]

The incidents I have cited are instances of the intrusion of matters which have not been properly 'worked up' or transformed for orderly and easeful use within the encounter. When an encounter is thoroughly and officially permeated by particular externally based social attri-

43. C. H. Cooley, *Human Nature and the Social Order* (New York: Scribner's, 1922), pp. 259–60.

butes, as in the interaction between a private and an officer, or between a commoner and royalty, it is possible for the activity of the
encounter to be pursued without distracting consideration being
given to the social distinctions. In such a context, however, an unanticipated event which could be taken to imply status equality can
function as a sign situation, suddenly throwing into doubt a ranking
that has been unthinkingly taken for granted. This is part of the problem of *lèse-majesté*, which characteristically arises when royalty in-
dulges in games of skill, but is not a problem for royalty alone. For
example, we have the engaging description by W. F. Whyte of bowling among the Nortons, who were members of the street-corner
society that Mr Whyte made famous.[44] Here we are told of the various
social pressures that players introduce so that their relative skill rank
as bowlers will not be too inconsistent with their social rank in the
clique at large.

5. *Integrations*. As suggested, in any focused gathering there are
likely to be officially irrelevant matters that actively draw the concern and attention of the participants, giving rise to tension. In addition, there are likely to be matters that are currently held back by
selective inattention but would cause tension were they introduced
pointedly. By contributing especially apt words and deeds, it is
possible for a participant to blend these embarrassing matters
smoothly into the encounter in an officially accepted way, even while
giving support to the prevailing order. Such acts are the structural
correlates of charm, tact, or presence of mind. These acts provide a
formula through which a troublesome event can be redefined and its
reconstituted meaning integrated into the prevailing definition of the
situation, or a means of partially redefining the prevailing encounter,
or various combinations of both.

In any case, by these means dysphoria can be intentionally reduced.
I shall refer here to the integration or blending-in of tension-produc-
ing materials. What is involved is a kind of grounding of disruptive
forces, an alteration of a frame for the benefit of those who are
framed by it. For example: when a pigeon flew in the window of
Beatrice Lillie's New York apartment, she is said to have interrupted
her conversation long enough to glance up and inquire, 'Any
messages?'[45] Another example may be cited from the predicament of

44. W. F. Whyte, 'Bowling and Social Ranking', *Street Corner Society* (University of Chicago Press, revised editn, 1955), pp. 14–25.

45. Cited in the *Observer*, 21 September 1958, p. 15.

a housemother engaged in looking after acting-out institutionalized children, one aspect of her job being to keep the participants contained in their encounters, in part by preventing sign situations from releasing into the encounter feelings of sibling rivalry theretofore held in uneasy check:

Most activities involving our Housemother were extremely loaded with special risks. This was due to violent sibling rivalry tensions which exploded around her with much greater volatility than around other female staff, because of the obvious impact of her mother role. Any situation in which she was the central figure in the group activity had, therefore, to be handled with hair trigger sensitivity on her part. On one occasion, for example, she started to read a story to the group while they were munching their 'treat' upon return from school. She was sitting on the couch and the group was ranged on either side of her when suddenly bickering broke out about who had the right 'to sit right next to Emmy' – Larry, who was on her right, was viciously slapped by Danny, who in turn began to draw fire from Mike, Andy, and Bill. Group riot looked imminent when Emmy suddenly broke in with 'Hey, wait a minute – I've got an idea. I'll read campfire style.' 'Campfire style – what's that?' Danny asked as they temporarily stopped their milling and mauling of each other. 'Oh, I'll be in the centre and you'll make a circle around me – that'll make me the campfire and each of you will be the same distance away.' This worked out to divert them from their feuding for that afternoon's story anyway.[46]

Here we can note a very curious aspect of social interaction: desire to do the right thing and an appreciation of what should be done run well ahead of participants' capacity to do it. Individuals are always making an effort to assimilate matters through techniques that are not effective; it is after the occasion, at a time of recollection in tranquility, that they hit upon the phrase or action that would have been completely effective in the situation. Furthermore, an effort at integration that does not succeed ordinarily leaves matters in a worse state than before the task was attempted. Such failure means either that the definition of the situation is altered in a way that increases its unacceptability to participants, or that the participants must now try to disattend something to which their attention has been explicitly directed. Interestingly enough, because such an unsuccessful act is damaging, the actor is in a position of guilt; to be considerate of his now delicate position, others in the encounter usually make some

46. Fritz Redl and David Wineman, *Controls from Within* (Glencoe: The Free Press, 1952), p. 104.

effort to affect a little sign that the act has been successful, and this need to protect the offender can further alienate them from spontaneous involvement in the prescribed situation.

Again the situation of the physically handicapped provides important data, illustrating that when a very evident basis of re-identification must be treated as irrelevant (adherence to the transformation rules being under great strain) then either a failure to integrate the suppressed issue or an effort to do so may equally lead to intense uneasiness, a situation for which there is no solution. Wanting to reject an image of self as abnormal and wanting to keep others at a distance from his problem, the handicapped person may none the less feel that the tension will be intolerable unless he openly alludes to his condition and 'breaks the ice'.[47]

Minor integrations, or an attempt to perform them, occur constantly during conversational encounters, as when participants attempt to shift from a topic that has dried up or become dangerous to a new one that is calculated to provide safe supplies for a moment; in fact, etiquette books give explicit attention to the art of changing topics. Similarly, in order to get away with obtruding the self upon the interaction, either as speaker or as subject matter, the individual employs countless assimilating ruses to disguise the intrusion. Thus, we have a set of standard opening phrases – 'The way I see it . . .' 'In my opinion . . .' 'Well, I don't know anything about that sort of thing, but I've always felt that . . .' 'Well, if you ask me . . .' 'The same thing happened to me, I was . . .' – whereby the willing talker provides what he takes to be a smooth connection between the established content of the encounter and a tale involving self.

Often, during an encounter, a participant will sense that a discrepancy has arisen between the image of himself that is part of the official definition of the situation and the image of himself that seems to have just been expressed by minor untoward events in the interaction. He then senses that the participants in the encounter are having to sup-

47. See, for example, R. K. White, B. A. Wright, and T. Dembo, 'Studies in Adjustment to Visible Injuries: Evaluation of Curiosity by the Injured', *Journal of Abnormal and Social Psychology*, 43 (1948), pp. 13–28, especially pp. 25–7. I would like to add that an interesting difference in class culture is seen here. In the urban working class, a boy with a physical or social peculiarity may have constant recognition of this shortcoming built into the nickname by which he is addressed; certain kinds of tension are therefore unlikely to build up. A middle-class youth with the same stigma is likely to be greeted more tactfully, but sometimes with more tension.

press awareness of the new version of him, with consequent tension. (While ordinarily this new image of him is less favorable than the initial official one, the opposite can easily occur.) At such times, the individual is likely to try to integrate the incongruous events by means of apologies, little excuses for self, and disclaimers; through the same acts, incidentally, he also tries to save his face. This may easily be observed by examining situations in which minor failures are constantly generated, for example, in games such as bowling. After making a bad shot, and while turning from the alley to face the others, the player is likely to display a facial gesture expressing that the shot was not a fair or serious measure of the player's skill and that the others, therefore, need not alter or doubt their prior evaluation of him.

During encounters, the individual is obliged to try to cope with incidents by spontaneously treating them as if they had not occurred, or by integrating them as best he can into the official definition of the situation, or by merely sustaining tension without departing physically from the situation. Once an individual is ready to be governed by this morality of interaction, others can exploit matters by intentionally tampering with the frame, introducing at his expense references and acts which are difficult to manage.[48] An apt identification of this process is provided in a novel by Chandler Brossard. A girl called Grace is leaving after a visit to the summer cottage of a friend, Harry. There are two other guests, Max and Blake. Grace has just terminated a relationship with one man, who has already departed, and has initiated a new one with Blake, who is the narrator:

'Thanks for a fine time, Harry,' Grace said, taking his hand.
'I'm sorry you're leaving so soon,' he said. 'Come again next week end.'
'So long, Max.'
'So long, baby. Stay out of trouble.'
I carried her bag to the taxi, and the driver put it in the back of the car. She got in and closed the door. She put her face to the open window and I kissed her.
'Call me tonight,' I said.
'I will.'
The cab drove off and I walked back to the house. Max was lying on the couch listening to a ball game.
'That was a very sweet scene, Blake,' he said, talking as though he knew I had kissed Grace good-by.

48. Such acts are difficult to sanction harshly without further increasing the difficulty caused to the encounter.

'Glad you liked it.'

'Good old Max,' said Harry. 'Always on the make for a situation. He feels frustrated if he doesn't lay at least one situation a day.'[49]

The phenomenon of 'making' a situation, is not, of course, restricted to New York hipsters. Jane Austen provides a contrast, illustrating at the same time how the structure of a focused gathering itself can be introduced conversationally as a means of attacking the frame and discomfiting participants:

They stood for some time without speaking a word; and then she began to imagine that their silence was to last through the two dances, and at first was resolved not to break it; till suddenly fancying that it would be the greater punishment to her partner to oblige him to talk, she made some slight observation on the dance. He replied, and was again silent. After a pause of some minutes, she addressed him a second time with – 'It is *your* turn to say something now, Mr Darcy. *I* talked about the dance, and *you* ought to make some kind of remark on the size of the room, or the number of couples.'

He smiled, and assured her that whatever she wished him to say should be said.

'Very well. That reply will do for the present. Perhaps by and by I may observe that private balls are much pleasanter than public ones. But *now* we may be silent.'

'Do you talk by rule, then, while you are dancing?'

'Sometimes. One must speak a little, you know. It would look odd to be entirely silent for half an hour together; and yet for the advantage of *some*, conversation ought to be so arranged, as that they may have the trouble of saying as little as possible.'[50]

It may be added that 'making' the situation can become culturally elaborated: the exemplary tales by which members of disadvantaged groups sustain themselves usually contain a few mots, squelches, or ripostes made under circumstances that leave their targets no satisfactory comeback.[51]

49. Chandler Brossard, *Who Walk in Darkness* (New York: New Directions, 1952), p. 184.

50. *Pride and Prejudice*, ch. 18. I am indebted to an unpublished paper by Stephanie Rothman for this quotation.

51. See E. Goffman, 'On Face-Work', *Psychiatry*, 18 (1955), pp. 213–31, 'Making Points – The Aggressive Use of Face-Work', pp. 221–2. A useful statement, presented in terms of destroying another's possibility of control, may be found in Tom Burns, 'The Forms of Conduct', *American Journal of Sociology*, 64 (1958), pp. 142–3.

Perhaps the situations most likely to be 'made' by someone present are those where there is a special reason why a participant's non-relevant identity should be very much on everyone's mind, and where the excluded identity does not particularly threaten the possessor. For example, in our society, newly engaged couples attending small social parties are often the object of 'well-meaning' quips and sallies by which references to their on-coming change in status are jokingly woven into the conversation. The female member of the couple may offer those present further reasons for raillery. She is about to enjoy a relatively full change in status in what can be defined as a favorable direction, and her past non-married status therefore ceases to be one about which others are obliged to suppress concern.[52] Furthermore, since this is the time when males present could least be suspected of attempting to initiate a sexual relationship with her, they can bestow mock sexual advances on her, using her as an object through which to vent concern that must be suppressed about other females present. (The host's wife may also be employed in this manner.)

There are, of course, other situations where an individual is lightly caught in the cross-fire between two of his statuses. In some rural communities in Western Europe, a boy confirms the seriousness of his relationship with a girl by escorting her to weddings to which either or both have been invited. At the same time, there is the rule that immediate members of the bride's and groom's families should act together during the occasion, being seated somewhat apart from other guests. The girl friend or boy friend of any youthful member of this wedding group must therefore be found an escort who 'stands in' for the real thing, although at a time when everyone is taking careful note of who came with whom. The stand-in is often a 'safe' friend of the family, selected to ensure no misunderstanding on the part of others. It is understandable then that he (or she) will be fair game for quips and jokes: the implicit definition of oneself as the affianced of the other is established by the nature of the social occasion, and yet this definition is exactly what the various parties concerned must show they set no store by and believe no one else does either.

There are many settings in which an unstable division between officially relevant and non-relevant worlds leads someone present to attempt to make the situation. Workers are often required to sustain

52. A somewhat similar analysis can be made of all forms of 'hazing'. See E. Goffman, *The Presentation of Self in Everyday Life* (Allen Lane The Penguin Press, 1969), p. 154.

a task-oriented mutual activity in a context that is thoroughly imbued with claims on their identity which they must disavow, so that everywhere they turn a world that must be suppressed is thrust upon them. For example, a crew of carpenters called in after school hours to work amongst seats that can no longer hold them are likely to pass jokes about teachers; work in a church or cathedral may be 'made' in the same way. In a rural community, I have observed the same kind of joking on the part of three men helping to unload lumber for the local coffin-maker, and on the part of a large work crew of shepherds engaged in the annual task of castrating young rams, the standard joke here being to grab the youngest member of the crew and make as if to place his body in the appropriate position for receiving the shears.

Obviously, in some cases, these redefining acts reduce the general level of tension, even if at the cost of someone's discomfort, and therefore become difficult to distinguish from well-intentioned efforts to integrate distracting considerations.

6. *Flooding Out*. I have considered incidents, their integration, and the making of situations; a further concept can now be mentioned. It has so far been argued that the transformation rules of an encounter oblige the participant to withhold his attention and concern from many potential matters of consideration, and that he is likely to feign such inattention when he cannot spontaneously manifest it. Evidence of this actual or feigned conformity comes to us from his manner, especially his facial expression, for manner provides the fluid field upon which the collective affective style of the encounter is intimately impressed. The participant's visible emotional state, then, will have to be in tune and tempo with the melody sustained in the interaction.

It is apparent, however, that under certain circumstances the individual may allow his manner to be inundated by a flow of affect that he no longer makes a show of concealing. The matter in which he has been affecting disinvolvement suddenly becomes too much for him, and he collapses, if only momentarily, into a person not mobilized to sustain an appropriate expressive role in the current interaction; he *floods out*. Whether the individual bursts out crying or laughing, whether he erupts into open anger, shame, impatience, boredom, or anguish, he radically alters his general support of the interaction; he is momentarily 'out of play'.[53] Since the individual has been active in

53. Goffman, 'Embarrassment', p. 267. This paper deals with one chief form of flooding out, embarrassment.

some social role up to this time, sustaining the frame around the encounter, his flooding out constitutes one type of 'breaking frame'. A common example of flooding out occurs when an individual finds he can no longer 'keep a straight face' and bursts out laughing.[54]

It is commonly thought that a sharp explosive expression – a flooding out – on the part of a participant will clear the air and reduce tension, but this is by no means always so. When an individual floods out, his defection is often studiously overlooked by the remaining participants and even, a moment later, by the offender himself. And when this suppression, this effortful non-perception occurs, a new distractive element has been added to the context of the encounter, increasing the amount of attended-to-material that must be treated as if not attended, and hence, by definition, increasing the tension level. Contrary to first impressions, then, a flooding out is often likely to consistitute an incident.

It should be apparent that persons will differ greatly in their capacity to sustain tension without exhibiting it and without flooding out. This difference in degree of poise is to be accounted for at least in part by differences in group affiliation: middle-class American four-years-olds will sometimes blush and wriggle away when they are merely looked at, whereas Victorian *grandes dames* are reported to have been able to maintain poise under quite disastrous conditions.

It seems characteristic of teams that perform specialized work under pressure that the members develop a capacity to keep from mind, or to appear unmindful of, happenings which would cause those with less experience to flood out. Surgical teams in action provide nice illustrations, since they are obliged to maintain a single frame or perspective, a medical definition of the situation, that applies in a detailed way to a great number of minor events occurring during the task encounter; and yet the tasks performed in surgery can easily introduce lively reminders that other definitions of the situation are possible. Thus, when a small artery is accidentally cut and the blood shoots up into the face of an assistant, describing a pretty arc in doing so, attention may in fact not shift from the work that is being

54. As a reminder that encounters involve psychobiological processes, there is the often-noted fact that under conditions of fatigue individuals seem likely to find almost anything funny enough to cause them to flood out of the frame in which they have been. See, for example, G. Bateson, 'The Position of Humor in Human Communication', in H. von Foerster, ed., *Cybernetics*, Transactions of The Ninth (1952) Conference (New York: Josiah Macy, Jr. Foundation, 1953), p. 18.

done except to tie off the 'bleeder'.[55] Similarly, when a small group of confirmed lovers of modern chamber music gather to listen to an informal, live, first performance of a local composer's quartet, everyone present can be counted on not to smile, giggle, or look quizzically about for definitional cues. An unschooled audience, however, would find great difficulty in drawing a line between the end of the tuning up and the beginning of the first movement, that is, between the tuning frame and the performing frame; its members would also feel less secure in taking the music seriously than in expressing disbelief. Unschooled audiences would, therefore, be unlikely to contain themselves on such an occasion.

Under what circumstances is flooding out likely, and when is it unlikely?

Common sense leads us to imagine that as the tension level increases, so the likelihood of flooding out increases, until the breaking point is reached and flooding out is inevitable. The work required of the transformation rules becomes intolerable, and there follows either disorder or a new, more manageable definition of the situation. The imagery here is hydraulic and not entirely adequate, for common sense neglects some important social determinants of how much tension can be withstood before a flooding out occurs.

During occasions when the reputation of large organizations or persons of high station are at stake, any open admission that things are not what they seem may carry externally relevant consequences that no one wants to face, and so a great deal of tension may be doggedly contained. It is no accident that the fable of the invisible new clothes concerns an emperor; so much difficult disregard of nakedness – so much resistance to re-identification – could hardly be sustained for a less consequential figure. Similarly, where one person is another's mentor, flooding out may be felt to be out of the question, as when an officer trainee learns that officers never break ranks and fall out because of illness or exhaustion,[56] or when a father in a burning theater restrains himself from joining the general panic flight to the exits because he does not want his small son to see him lose self-control.[57] So, too, when large numbers of participants are in-

55. Writer's unpublished study of two surgery wards.

56. Simon Raven, 'Perish by the Sword: A Memoir of the Military Establishment', *Encounter*, 12 (1959), p. 38.

57. Cited by E. L. Quarantelli in 'A Study of Panic: Its Nature, Types, and Conditions' (unpublished Master's thesis, Department of Sociology, University of Chicago, 1953), p. 75, from a published account by C. B. Kelland.

volved, there may be difficulty in obtaining agreement on a concerted change in the definition of the situation. On the other hand, informality can be partly defined as a license to flood out on minor pretexts; in fact, during informal encounters of a few people, small amounts of tension may be purposely engineered just for the fun of being capsized by them. Such encounters seem to have hardly any boundary, and almost anything of an extraneous nature can penetrate into the interaction. Because of this, we tend to think of such encounters as being easy, natural, and relaxed.

Instead of simply following common-sense notions, then, we must drastically limit our generalizations: we can only say that given a focused gathering which includes a given number of participants of given social statuses interacting with a given level of formality and seriousness, then the stability of role performance will vary inversely with the tension level.

I have suggested that when an individual floods out, other participants may contagiously flood out, too, or treat the incident (whether spontaneously or self-consciously) as if it had not occurred. There is also a third way in which participants respond to an offender. Seeking a tolerable level of tension, they can openly alter the rules, redefining the situation around the plight of the offender, but treating him now *not as a participant but as a mere focus of attention* – in fact, as an involuntary performer. Examples are to be found in situations where individuals are purposely teased until they flood out or at least become trapped in a 'rise', thereby ensuring momentary easy involvement for the others, albeit in an encounter with new boundaries.[58]

58. An excellent general statement may be found in John Dollard, 'The Dozens: Dialect of Insult', *American Imago*, 1 (1939), pp. 3–25. (A prison version is reported by Alfred Hassler, *Diary of a Self-Made Convict* (Chicago: Regnery, 1954), pp. 126–7.) 'There is a "game" some of the boys "play" in here called "playing the dozens". I have no idea what the origin of the name can be, but the idea is that the participants try to make each other mad by hurling epithets. The first one to lose his temper loses the game. I listened in on one, and it stood my hair on end. The "players" vie with each other in combining the most obscene and insulting accusations against not only the opponent himself, but anyone for whose reputation he might conceivably have some regard. Mothers, sisters, wives, children all come under the ban, and the players explore possibilities of degraded behavior, generally sexual, of the most revolting nature.

'Quite frequently, both players lose their tempers, and actual fights are not unknown. Occasionally, a man will "play the dozens" with someone who has not experienced it before, and in such case the consequence can be serious. One man was knifed not long ago in just such an affair.'

Thus, in the Shetlandic community studied by the writer, women of almost any age seemed to find it difficult to sustain an explicit compliment with equanimity and perhaps were not expected to do so. When complimented, they would often cast their heads down modestly, or, in cases where the complimenting was meant to tease, would rush at their tormentors with arms flailing, in a joking and cooperative effort to disrupt the exchange.[59]

An individual may mildly flood out, for example, by blushing, and half-induce others to reconstitute the mutual activity but now with himself temporarily in the role of mere object of attention. His willingness to withdraw in this way is presumably compensated for by the briefness with which the others require him to be outside the encounter.

There is a special kind of 'free' flooding out that should be mentioned. When an alteration in official rules of irrelevance occurs, we can, perhaps, say, as Freud argued, that the 'energy' previously employed to 'bind' the suppressions can be set 'free'.[60] Further, the new rules of irrelevance – the new frame of reference – often provide a context in which it is especially difficult to maintain the previous suppressions. And so the participants flood out in regard to a definition of the situation that has just been displaced, it being safe to offend something no longer credited as reality. Typically, in such cases, we

---

See also Bateson and Mead, *Balinese Character* (New York: New York Academy of Sciences, 1942), discussion of teasing, pp. 148–9. A variation of the game of the 'dozens', the Italian game called *La Passatella*, played by male adults in cafés, is presented in detail in Roger Vailland's novel, *The Law*, trans. Peter Wiles (New York: Bantam Books, 1959), pp. 30–40, 46–52, 63. For a comment on cursing contests in India, see Robert Graves, *The Future of Swearing* (London: Kegan Paul, 1936), pp. 35–40.

59. E. Goffman, 'Communication Conduct in an Island Community' (unpublished Ph.D. dissertation, Department of Sociology, University of Chicago, 1953), p. 254.

60. See, for example, his analysis in *Wit and Its Relation to the Unconscious*. His argument, of course, is that once someone else has introduced the taboo material it becomes inessential to cathect its suppression, and this energy, now freed, is drained off in laughter and elation: 'Following our understanding of the mechanism of laughter we should be more likely to say that the cathexis utilized in the inhibition has now suddenly become superfluous and neutralized because a forbidden idea came into existence by way of auditory perception, and is, therefore, ready to be discharged through laughter.' (*The Basic Writings of Sigmund Freud*, p. 735). Freud, of course, saw the suppressive function as associated often with sexually tinged matters, instead of merely socially irrelevant properties that disrupt identity-images, one instance of which is the sexual.

get a special-sounding 'safe laughter'.[61] This kind of laughter can often be distinguished by sound and gesture from the explosive, escaped, or blurted-out kind which can represent a personal failure to contain oneself, and which others present try to overlook. Interestingly enough, a laugh can start out as an involuntary failure at suppression, receive confirmation from others present, contagiously leading to a general (although usually temporary) abandonment of the previous definition of the situation, and then end with a sound that is unguilty and free. The whole encounter can thus flood out. Further, a 'tipping' phenomenon can occur, with guilt for what they are about to do to the encounter for a time inhibiting those who are first to flood out, and freedom from responsibility facilitating the frame-break of those who flood out a moment later.

7. *Structure and Process*. We now may examine how the dynamics of interaction tie into its structure. During any encounter it is possible for a sub-set of participants to form a communicative byplay and, without ratifying their new mutual activity except among themselves, withdraw spontaneous involvement from the more inclusive encounter.[62] It is even possible for *all* the participants in a given encounter to join together to sustain a single, all-inclusive byplay, as when a team of workers momentarily slow up their work because of a particularly interesting bit of gossip. (It is also possible for 'self collusion' to occur, as when a discomfited person finds it necessary to swear to himself and utter a brief comment to himself, in the face of needing the release but having no one present with whom to share it.) Sometimes these byplays are carried on quite furtively; always the gestures through which they are sustained will be modulated so as to show a continued respect for the official or dominant encounter.

If an individual finds himself flooding out of an officially binding

61. R. F. Bales ('The Equilibrium Problem in Small Groups', p. 143, in T. Parsons, R. F. Bales and E. A. Shils, *Working Papers in the Theory of Action* (Glencoe: The Free Press, n.d.) suggests: 'We note joking and laughter so frequently at the end of meetings that they might almost be taken as a signal that the group has completed what it considers to be a task effort, and is ready for disbandment or a new problem. This last-minute activity completes a cycle of operations involving a successful solution both of the task problems and social-emotional problems confronting the group.'

If we assume that the experimental subjects Bales employed felt obliged to disattend considerations that might throw doubt on what they were being asked to do, then we can intepret their terminal flooding out as a form of safe laughter.

62. See Goffman, *The Presentation of Self*, 'Team Collusion', pp. 155–66.

encounter, one way in which he can handle his predicament is to enter into a more or less furtive byplay with one or two other participants. In this collusive encounter, a kind of ratification can be given to feelings and issues which have had to be suppressed in the dominant encounter. Unusable elements in the larger encounter can thus be removed by placing them at the center of a subordinate one. The byplay that results can realize among a small coalition of participants a congruence between official and spontaneous matters of concern that cannot be sustained by all of the participants.[63] Such draining action, while a threat to the official encounter, also provides a safety valve for it, for through the congenial world found in the byplay, the alienated participant can reassert control over himself.

As we might expect, upon the termination of an encounter in which much suppression has been needed, the ex-participants may immediately form into smaller groupings in which open expression of these tabooed matters becomes possible, giving rise not to byplays but rather to 'postplays'.[64]

While the affective bases of flooding out – joy, sorrow, fear, and so on – can vary, one emotion seems to have a special importance in the formation of tension-reducing byplays, namely, the moral shock that is evoked by witnessing improper acts. An example of such flooding out can often be observed when a well-meaning institutional psychiatrist attempts in the presence of a nurse to interview a mental patient who is, say, senile, mute, or paranoid. The psychiatrist's apparent sympathetic offer of a joint conversational world with the patient is at some point likely to fail to call forth 'appropriate' participant activity from the patient, and at such a point there is a strong tendency indeed for the psychiatrist to glance at the nurse in a collusive gesture of despair or derision. This sort of thing is found where-

63. A collusive byplay is not, however, inevitably euphoric for all its participants. An individual may feel obliged to engage in a byplay because of not wanting to reject the person who signals a desire to initiate one. The importuned person may then find himself under double tension, on the one hand in regard to the dominant encounter toward which he feels disloyal, and on the other in regard to the byplay in which he must appear to be spontaneously involved, although he is actually involved in his concern over the conflicting demands upon him.

64. This phenomenon is described, under the title 'Postconference Reactions', in a paper that provides a very thorough case history of the process of selective inattention and suppression, especially in regard to the management of tension during formal meetings. See S. E. Perry and G. N. Shea, 'Social Controls and Psychiatric Theory in a Ward Setting', *Psychiatry*, 20 (1957), pp. 221–47, especially pp. 243–4. Terminal laughter, described by Bales, is a related possibility.

ever one person tries in the presence of another to 'get to' a third person who is a recalcitrant or incompetent participant.

Since a collusive byplay provides a tempting means of reducing tension, certain additional patterns of behaviour are likely to be associated with it. One of these is eye-avoidance. When a person is just able to restrain himself from flooding out in laughter or tears, his 'catching the eye' of another may lead to involuntary byplay, especially when the other is known to be in the same predicament and to be someone with whom the individual can safely engage in the intimacies of a collusive exchange. A minor release by one member of the coalition can form a basis for the other to give way a little more, and this in turn can be fed back into the system until both parties have lost control of themselves, while neither feels he is quite responsible for what has happened. Thus, persons may avoid each other's eyes to avoid starting a process that might finish them as participants.

Another pattern takes the form of a kind of flooding in, instead of flooding out. There will often be persons in close proximity to a conversational encounter who, while not ratified as official participants, are none the less within easy hearing range of the talk and respond to this by maintaining a tactful look of inattention. When an incident occurs in this half-overheard encounter, especially a funny incident, the outsiders may find it impossible to sustain an appearance of involvement in their own official activity. During such moments, they may find themselves entering into collusive byplay with one or more participants, the resulting encounter cutting across the boundaries of the dominant one. For example, when a bus conductor finds that a passenger insists on disputing the fare or is too intoxicated to handle change properly, the conductor may in wry moral indignation collude with the next passenger in line, breaking down a barrier to do so. Similarly, when a number of persons find themselves in the same elevator, and are silent except for two or three who are openly carrying on a conversation, an appropriate remark on the part of one of the nonparticipants may collapse the boundary separating the participants from the nonparticipants.

I have suggested that tension generated in an encounter can be dealt with through actions involving the structure of the encounter: momentary reduction of a participant into a mere performer, collusive byplays, postplays. An important additional possibility must be mentioned.

When all the participants in an encounter together flood out, say, into laughter, very commonly the prior definition of the situation is resurrected after the outburst has passed. What seems to be involved is not an alteration of the transformation rules, followed by a re-alteration, a return to the initial formula, but rather a momentary abeyance of the dominant encounter while a subordinate one is allowed fleetingly to hold sway. The collusive byplay which results is as temporary as most but includes all the participants in the encounter. The possibility of maintaining a subordinate encounter, even while maintaining a dominant one, is pressed to its limits and burdened with a sudden task. Thus, individuals can collectively collapse as participants in a focused gathering but the next moment can set their collapse aside and dissociate themselves from it, returning to the prior world but with less tension. It is this dissociable collapse that typically occurs when situations are 'made' or tension-reducing integrations are attempted. And this, too, is what is usually involved when 'free' flooding out occurs.

Since the introduction of a tactful or hostile joke is likely to lead all the participants into a temporary new engagement if successful and into greater dysphoria if unsuccessful, we can understand that the right to make such efforts will not be randomly distributed among the participants of the encounter but that role differentiation will occur which places this venturesome function in special hands. This is especially true when the participants spend time together in a series of similar encounters. Thus, the right to 'make a joke of something' is often restricted to the ranking person present,[65] or to a subordinate playing the part of a fool[66] – a part that allows him to take liberties during interaction in exchange for his character. In either case, this redirecting influence can be accomplished without threatening to alter the sensed distribution of influence and power within the encounter. Where material is introduced that permanently alters the transformation rules, an even closer fit between manipulation and rank may be expected.

8. *Interaction Membrane*. It should now be evident that the concept of transformation rules does not cover all the facts. When the wider world passes through the boundary of an encounter and is worked into the interaction activity, more than a re-ordering or trans-

65. Rose Coser, 'Laughter Among Colleagues', *Psychiatry*, 23 (1960), pp. 81–95.
66. O. E. Klapp, 'The Fool as a Social Type', *American Journal of Sociology*, 55 (1949), pp. 157–62.

formation of pattern occurs. Something of an organic psychobiological nature takes place. Some of the potentially determinative wider world is easefully disattended; some is repressed; and some is suppressed self-consciously at the price of felt distraction. Where easeful disattention occurs, there will be no tendency to modify the transformation rules; where felt distraction occurs there will be pressure on the rulings. An incident endangers the transformation rules, not directly but by altering the psychic work that is being done by those who must interact in accordance with these rules.

In order to think more easily in these organic terms, an organic metaphor might be attempted. A living cell usually has a cell wall, a membrane, which cuts the cell off from components in its external milieu, ensuring a selective relation between them and the internal composition of the cell. The resilience and health of the cell is expressed in the capacity of its membrane to maintain a particular selective function. But unlike a set of transformation rules, a membrane does the actual work of filtering and does not merely designate that a selection from the external milieu is being maintained. Further, the membrane is subject to many threats, for it can sustain its work and its function over only a small range of changes in the external system.

If we think of an encounter as having a metaphorical membrane around it, we can bring our concerns into focus. We can see that the dynamics of an encounter will be tied to the functioning of the boundary-maintaining mechanisms that cut the encounter off selectively from wider worlds.[67] And we can begin to ask about the kinds of components in the encounter's external milieu that will expand or contract the range of events with which the encounter deals, and the kinds of components that will make the encounter resilient or destroy it.

BASES OF FUN

In this paper, we have come by stages to focus on the question of euphoria in encounters, arguing that euphoria arises when persons can spontaneously maintain the authorized transformation rules. We assume that participants will judge past encounters according to

67. A clear statement of this issue in terms of an 'external system', an 'internal system', and a boundary can be found in G. C. Homans, *The Human Group* (New York: Harcourt, Brace, 1950), pp. 86–94.

whether they were or were not easy to be in and will be much concerned to maximize euphoria, through, for example, integrative acts,
topic selection, and avoidance of encounters likely to be dysphoric.

But of course this tells us only in a very general way what people
do to ensure easeful interaction, for in pointing to the requirement
that spontaneous involvement must coincide with obligatory involvement, we are merely pushing the problem back one step. We still
must go on to consider what will produce this congruence for any
given encounter.

In concluding this paper, then, I would like to take a speculative
look at some of the conditions, once removed, that seem to ensure
easeful interaction. Again, there seems to be no better starting point
than what I labeled gaming encounters. Not only are games selected
and discarded on the basis of their ensuring euphoric interaction,
but, to ensure engrossment, they are also sometimes modified in a
manner provided for within their rules, thus giving us a delicate
tracer of what is needed to ensure euphoria. Instead of having to
generate an allocation of spontaneous involvement that coincides
with the transformation rules, it is possible to modify the transformation rules to fit the distribution and possibilities of spontaneous
involvement. The practices of 'balancing' teams, handicapping,
limiting participation to skill classes, or adjusting the betting limits,
all introduce sufficient malleability into the materials of the game to
allow the game to be molded and fashioned into a shape best suited
to hold the participants entranced. We can at last return, therefore,
to our original theme: fun in games.

There is a common-sense view that games are fun to play when the
outcome or pay-off has a good chance of remaining unsettled until
the end of play (even though it is also neccessary that play come to a
final settlement within a reasonable period of time). The practices
of balancing teams and of handicapping unmatched ones, and the
practice of judiciously interposing a randomizing element, 'pure luck'
(especially to the degree that perfect matching or handicapping is
not possible), all work to ensure that a prior knowledge of the attributes of the players will not render the outcome a foregone conclusion. On similar grounds, should the final score come to be predic-
table, as often happens near the end of the play, concession by the
loser is likely, terminating the action in the interests of both the play
and the gaming encounter.

To speak of the outcome as problematic, however, is, in effect, to

say that one must look to the play itself in order to discover how
things will turn out. The developing line built up by the alternating,
interlocking moves of the players can thus maintain sole claim upon
the attention of the participants, thereby facilitating the game's
power to constitute the current reality of its players and to engross
them. We can thus understand one of the social reasons why cheaters
are resented; by locating the power of determining the outcome of
the play in the arrangements made by one player, cheating, like mismatching, destroys the reality-generating power of the game.[68] (Of
course, whereas the mismatching of teams prevents a play world
from developing, the discovery that someone is cheating punctures
and deflates a world that has already developed.)

But this analysis is surely not enough. In games of pure chance,
such as flipping coins, there would never be a problem of balancing
sides, yet, unless such other factors as money bets are carefully added,
mere uncertainty of outcome is not enough to engross the players.

Another possibility is that games give the players an opportunity
to exhibit attributes valued in the wider social world, such as dexter-
ity, strength, knowledge, intelligence, courage, and self-control.
Externally relevant attributes thus obtain official expression within
the milieu of an encounter. These attributes could even be earned
within the encounter, to be claimed later outside it.

Again, this alone is not enough, for mismatched teams allow the
better player to exhibit all kinds of capacities. He, at least, should be
satisfied. Still, we know that, whatever his actual feelings, he is not
likely to admit to getting much satisfaction out of this kind of gaming
and is, in fact, quite likely to find himself bored and unengrossed in
the play.

But if we combine our two principles – problematic outcome and
sanctioned display – we may have something more valid. A successful game would then be one which, first, had a problematic outcome
and then, within these limits, allowed for a maximum possible display of externally relevant attributes.

This dual theme makes some sense. A good player who is unop-

68. Harvey Sacks has suggested to me that game etiquette may oblige those
who discover a cheater to warn him secretly so that he is enabled to desist or
withdraw without totally breaking up the play. Presumably, an open accusation
of cheating would be even more destructive of the play than the knowledge on the
part of some of the players that cheating is occurring. That which is threatened
by cheating is that which determines the form that control of cheating can take.

posed in displaying his powers may give the impression of too openly making claims; he would be acting contrary to the rules of irrelevance which require him to forego attending to many of his externally relevant social attributes. But as long as his efforts are called forth in the heat of close competition, they are called forth by the interaction itself and not merely for show. Uncertainty of outcome gives the player a shield behind which he can work into the interaction attributes that would threaten the membrane surrounding the encounter if openly introduced.

How far can we generalize this explanation? First we must see that this conception of a dual principle leads us back to a consideration of betting games and the efforts of those around a table to locate a euphoria function. If the participants perceive that the betting is very low relative to their financial capacities, then interest in money itself cannot penetrate the encounter and enliven it. Interest in the game may flag; participants may fail to 'take it seriously'. On the other hand, if the players feel that the betting is high in relation to their income and resources, then interest may be strangled, a participant in a play flooding out of the gaming encounter into an anxious private concern for his general economic welfare.[69] A player in these circumstances is forced to take the game 'too seriously'.

When players at the beginning of play give thought to an appropriate scale of stakes, they are seeking for that kind of screen behind which an interest in money can seep into the game. This is one reason for restricting the game to persons who, it is felt, can afford to lose roughly the same amount. We can similarly understand the tendency for the level of bets to be raised part way through the gaming, since by then the game itself has had a chance to grasp the players and inure them against what they previously considered too worrisome a loss.

We also see that the notion of taking a game too seriously or not seriously enough does not quite fit our notions of the contrast between recreational 'unserious' activity and workaday 'serious' activity. The issue apparently is not whether the activity belongs to

69. It is interesting that in daily life when individuals personally convey or receive what is for them large amounts of money they often make a little joke about money matters. Presumably, the integrity of the exchange encounter is threatened by concern about the funds, and the joke is an effort to assimilate this source of distraction to the interaction in progress, thereby (hopefully) reducing tension. In any case, to demonstrate that the money is not being treated 'seriously' is presumably to imply that the encounter itself is the important thing.

the recreational sphere or the work sphere, but whether external pulls upon one's interest can be selectively held in check so that one can become absorbed in the encounter as a world in itself. The problem of too-serious or not-serious-enough arises in gaming encounters not because a game is involved but because an encounter is involved.

Financial status is not the only fundamental aspect of a person's life which can enter through the membrane of an encounter and enliven or spoil the proceedings. Physical safety, for example, seems to be another. In children's play activities, risk to the physical integrity of the body is often introduced, again on a carefully graded not-too-much-not-too-little basis. For example, slides must be steep enough to be a challenge, yet not so steep as to make an accident too likely: a little more risk than can be easily handled seems to do the trick. (Adult sports such as skiing seem to be based on the same principle – a means of creating tension in regard to physical safety is here integrated into the play activity, giving rise to merriment.)[70] All of this has been stated by Fritz Redl in his discussion of the 'ego-supporting' functions of successful games:

> I would like to list a few of the things that must happen for a 'game' to 'break down'. It breaks down if it is not fun any more; that means if certain gratification guarantees, for the sake of which individuals were lured into it, stop being gratifying. There are many reasons why that may happen. It breaks down, too, if it is not safe any more, that is, when the risks or the dangers an individual exposes himself to in the game outweigh whatever gratification he may derive from it. By safe, I mean internally and externally. The actual risks and the physical strain or the fear of hurt may become too great or the fear of one's own passivity may become too great. This is why, by choice, children sometimes do not allow themselves to play certain games, because they are afraid of their own excitation or they know that the danger of loss of self-control in this activity is so seductive and so great that they would rather not play. In fact, some of the mechanisms of games seem to be built to guarantee gratification, but they also guarantee security against one's own superego pressures or against the outside dangers. Again, a game breaks down when the 'as if' character cannot be maintained, or when the reality proximity is too great, and this may vary from game to game. There are some games that stop being fun

70. Roger Caillois, op. cit., p. 107, speaks here of 'games based on the pursuit of vertigo'. He says, 'The question is less one of overcoming fear than of voluptuously experiencing fear, a shudder, a state of stupor that momentarily causes one to lose self-control.' See also his *Les Jeux et les Hommes* (Paris: Gallimard, 1958), pp. 45–51, where he elaborates his discussion of games based on *ilinx*.

when they get too fantastic and there is not enough similarity to a real competitive situation; there are other games which stop being fun the other way around. If one comes too close to reality, then the activity may lose its game character, as do some games that are too far from reality. Where is too far away or too close? This is the question for which I do not know the answer. [71]

It is possible to go on and see in games a means of infusing or integrating into gaming encounters many different socially significant externally based matters. This seems to be one reason why different cultural milieux favor different kinds of games, and some historical changes in the equipment of a game appear to respond to social changes in the milieu in which the game is played.[72] And apart from the equipment itself, there is the issue of the wider social position of the contending players. Thus, for example, the clash of football teams on a playing field can provide a means by which the antagonism between the two groups represented by the teams may be allowed to enter an encounter in a controlled manner and to be given expression.[73] We can then predict that, at least as far as spectators are concerned, two teams drawn from the same social grouping may produce a conflict that falls flat, and two teams drawn from groupings openly opposed to each other may provide incidents during which so much externally based hostility flows into the mutual activity of the sporting encounter as to burst the membrane surrounding it, leading to riots, fights, and other signs of a breakdown in order. All this is suggested by Max Gluckman in his discussion of British football, where he attempts to explain why league teams can represent different schools, towns, and regions, but with much more difficulty different religious groupings and different social classes:

A similar situation might be found in school matches. We know that the

71. Fritz Redl, discussing Gregory Bateson's 'The Message "This is Play"', in Bertram Schaffner, ed., *Group Processes*, Transactions of the Second (1955) Conference (New York: The Josiah Macy, Jr Foundation, 1956), pp. 212–13. See also Redl's 'The Impact of Game-Ingredients on Children's Play Behavior', in Bertram Schaffner, ed., *Group Processes*, Transactions of the Fourth (1957) Conference (New York: The Josiah Macy, Jr Foundation, 1959), pp. 33–81.

72. See, for example, K. M. Colby's treatment of the changing character of chessmen in 'Gentlemen, The Queen!' *Psychoanalytic Review*, 40 (1953), pp. 144–8.

73. In this connection, see the functional interpretation of North Andamanese peace-making ceremonies in A. R. Radcliffe-Brown, *The Andaman Islanders* (Glencoe: The Free Press, 1948), pp. 134–5, 238 ff.

unity and internal loyalty of schools is largely built up by formalized competition in games with other schools – and I should expect this system to
work well as long as each school mainly played other schools of the same
type as itself. What would happen if public schools became involved in
contests with secondary modern schools? Would the whole national back-
ground of divergence in opportunity, prospects, and privilege, embitter the
game till they ceased to serve their purpose of friendly rivalry? Is it only
because Oxford and Cambridge can produce better teams than the pro-
vincial universities that they confine their rivalry in the main to contests
between themselves?[74]

The social differences, then, between the two supporting audiences
for the teams must be of the kind that can be tapped without breaking the barrel. It may be, however, that the same can be said about
any major externally based experience common to members of an
audience. A stage play that does not touch on issues relevant to the
audience is likely to fall flat, and yet staged materials can be pressed
to a point where they insufficiently disguise the realities on which
they dwell, causing the audience to be moved too much. Thus, realis-
tic plays put on for unsophisticated audiences are felt by some to be
in bad taste, to 'go too far', or to 'come too close to home' – as was
the feeling, so I was informed, when *Riders to the Sea* was staged
for a Shetland audience. What has been called 'symbolic distance'
must be assured. A membrane must be maintained that will control
the flow of externally relevant sentiments into the interaction. Interestingly enough, the same effect can be seen in the judgment adult
audiences make in watching their children use sacred materials for
purposes of play, as Caillois points out in discussing the fact that
games are not merely current residues of past realities:

74. Max Gluckman, 'How Foreign Are You?', the *Listener*, 15 January 1959,
p. 102. Of course, the Olympic games bring teams of different nationalities against
each other, but the heavy institutionalization of these competitions seems to be
exactly what is needed to strengthen the membrane within which these games are
played; and, in spite of the dire implication, opposing Olympic teams do occasionally fight. P. R. Reid (op. cit., p. 64), suggests a similar argument in his
discussion of the wall games played by British prisoners of war at Colditz: 'The
Poles, and later the French when they arrived, were always interested spectators.
Although we had no monopoly of the courtyard, they naturally took to their rooms
and watched the game from the windows. They eventually put up sides against the
British and games were played against them, but these were not a success.
Tempers were lost and the score became a matter of importance, which it never
did in an " all-British " game.' See also George Orwell, 'The Sporting Spirit',
in *Shooting an Elephant* (New York: Harcourt, Brace, 1950), pp. 151–5.

These remarks are no less valid for the sacred than for the profane. The katcinas are semidivinites, the principal objects of worship among the Pueblo Indians of New Mexico; this does not prevent the same adults who worship them and incarnate them in their masked dances from making dolls resembling them for the amusement of their sons. Similarly, in Catholic countries, children currently play at going to Mass, at being confirmed, at marriage and funerals. Parents permit this at least as long as the imitation remains a respectful one. In black Africa the children make masks and rhombs in the same way and are punished for the same reasons, if the imitation goes too far and becomes too much of a parody or a sacrilege.[75]

It seems, then, that in games and similar activities disguises must be provided which check, but do not stop, the flow of socially significant matters into the encounter. All this goes beyond my earlier statement that the material character of game equipment is not relevant. The game-relevant meanings of the various pieces of the game equipment are in themselves a useful disguise, for behind these meanings the sentimental, material, and esthetic value of the pieces can steal into the interaction, infusing it with tones of meaning that have nothing to do with the logic of the game but something to do with the pleasure of the gaming encounter; the traditional concern in Japan about the quality of equipment used to play *Go* is an extreme example. In this way, too, perhaps, the conversation and cuisine in a restaurant can, if good enough, not only blot out a humble setting, but also, in elegant establishments, allow us a deepened identification with the cost of the décor, the command in the service, and the social status of groups at the other tables – an identification we would not allow ourselves were the process not disguised. And it seems that the malleability of game arrangements – choice of games, sides, handicaps, bets – allows for the fabrication of exactly the right amount of disguise.

But here we have a theme that echoes the doctrine that has been built around projective testing, namely, that the ambiguity and malleability of test material allow subjects to structure it according to their own propensity, to express quite personal 'loaded' themes because the materials are sufficiently removed from reality to allow the subject to avoid seeing what he is doing with them. A discontinuity with the world is achieved even while a connection with it is established. Of course, these tests are usually directed to one subject and his world, as opposed to an encounter with many individuals in it, but the presence of the tester focusing his attention on the sub-

75. Caillois, 'Unity of Play', p. 97.

ject's response does in a way supply the conditions of a two-person encounter.

A glance at the literature on projective devices encourages us to continue along this tack. Take for example the beautiful work of Erikson on play therapy published in 1937.[76] He describes children who cannot bring themselves to talk about their troubles – in fact, may even be too young to do so. The affect attached to the suppressed and repressed materials would rupture any membrane around any mutual or individual activity that alluded to this material. In some cases these constraints block any verbal communication. But by allowing the child to construct play configurations out of doll-like objects that are somewhat removed from the reality projected on them, the child feels some relief, some ease; and he does so through the process of infusing his painful concerns into the local situation in a safely transformed manner.

Once the special relevance of projective testing is granted, we need not be bound by formal test materials, but can include any situation where an individual can permit himself to interact by virtue of a disguise, in fact, transformation rules that he is allowed to create. Fromm-Reichmann provides an example:

> Perhaps my interest began with the young catatonic woman who broke through a period of completely blocked communication and obvious anxiety by responding when I asked her a question about her feeling miserable: She raised her hand with her thumb lifted, the other four fingers bent towards her palm, so that I could see only the thumb, isolated from the four hidden fingers. I interpreted the signal with, 'That lonely?' in a sympathetic tone of voice. At this, her facial expression loosened up as though in great relief and gratitude, and her fingers opened. Then she began to tell me about herself by means of her fingers, and she asked me by gestures to respond in kind. We continued with this finger conversation for one or two weeks, and as we did so, her anxious tension began to decrease and she began to break through her noncommunicative isolation; and subsequently she emerged altogether from her loneliness.[77]

In both these cases what we see is an individual himself determining the kind of veil that will be drawn over his feelings while in communication with another. The system of etiquette and reserve that members of every group employ in social intercourse would seem

76. Erik Homburger [Erikson], 'Configurations in Play – Clinical Notes', *The Psychoanalytic Quarterly*, 6 (1937), pp. 139–214.

77. Frieda Fromm-Reichmann, 'Loneliness', *Psychiatry*, 22 (1959), p. 1.

to function in the same way, but in this case the disguise is socially standardized; it is applied by the individual but not tailored by himself to his own particular needs.

In psychotherapeutic intervention with greatly withdrawn patients, the therapist may have to agree to the patient's using a very heavy disguise, but in psychotherapy with 'neurotics', we may see something of the opposite extreme. In the psychoanalytical doctrine of transference and the psychoanalytical rule of free association, we meet the notion that a membrane can be established that is so diaphanous and yet so tough that any externally related feeling on the part of the patient can be activated and infused into the encounter without destroying the doctor-patient encounter. This is facilitated, of course, by the professional arrangement that separates the analytical couch from home life and home authorities.[78] The extension of this tell-all doctrine to group psychotherapy merely moves matters more in the direction of the kind of encounter considered in this paper.

This view of the function of disguise allows us to consider the phenomenon of 'subversive ironies'. One of the most appealing ways in which situations are 'made' can be found in times and places of stress where matters that are extremely difficult to bear and typically excluded by the official transformation rules are introduced lightly and ironically. The classic case is 'gallows humour'. In concentration camps, for example, turnips were sometimes called 'German pineapples',[79] fatigue drill, 'geography'.[80] In a mental hospital, a patient may express to other patients his feelings about the place by referring to the medical and surgical building with conscious irony as the 'hos-

78. See Melanie Klein, 'The Psycho-Analytic Play Technique: its history and significance', in Klein *et al.*, *New Directions in Psycho-Analysis* (London: Tavistock, 1955), p. 6: 'More important still, I found that the transference situation – the backbone of the psycho-analytic procedure – can only be established and maintained if the patient is able to feel that the consulting-room or the play-room, indeed the whole analysis, is something separate from his ordinary home life. For only under such conditions can he overcome his resistances against experiencing and expressing thoughts, feelings, and desires, which are incompatible with convention, and in the case of children felt to be in contrast to much of what they have been taught.' Perhaps, then, an ocean voyage is fun not because it cuts us off from ordinary life but because, in being apparently cut off from ordinary life, we can afford to experience certain aspects of it.

79. Eugen Kogon, *The Theory and Practice of Hell* (New York: Berkley Publishing Corp., n.d.), p. 108.

80. ibid., p. 103.

pital', thereby establishing the rest of the institution as a different kind of place.[81] In general, these subversive ironies would seem to 'come off' when they open the way for some expression of feeling that is generated in the institutional situation at large but disguise what is being expressed sufficiently to ensure the orderliness of the particular encounter.

Within the same perspective, we can consider the functions of indirection in informal social control. For example, when a member of a work group begins to threaten informal work quotas by producing too much, we can follow the actions of his fellow workers who, perhaps unwilling to express directly their resentment and their desire for control, may employ a game of 'bringing' or 'piling' through which the non-conformist is brought back into line under the guise of being the butt of a joke.[82]

Whatever the interaction, then, there is this dual theme: the wider world must be introduced, but in a controlled and disguised manner. Individuals can deal with one another face to face because they are ready to abide by rules of irrelevance, but the rules seem to exist to let something difficult be quietly expressed as much as to exclude it entirely from the scene. Given the dangers of expression, a disguise may function not so much as a way of concealing something as a way of revealing as much of it as can be tolerated in an encounter. We fence our encounters in with gates; the very means by which we hold off a part of reality can be the means by which we can bear introducing it.

As a final step, I would like to trace the same dual theme in sociability, in occasions such as parties, which form a structured setting for many comings-together during an evening.

81. Writer's study of a mental hospital. A systematic treatment of patient joking in mental hospitals can be found in Rose Coser, 'Some Social Functions of Laughter', *Human Relations*, 12 (1959), pp. 171–82. Somewhat similar practices are reported at length in a study of brain-damage cases held for surgery in a medical hospital: Edwin Weinstein and Robert Kahn, *Denial of Illness* (Springfield: Charles Thomas, 1955), ch. 16, 'The Language of Denial'.

82. See F. J. Roethlisberger and W. J. Dickson, *Management and the Worker* (Cambridge: Harvard University Press, 1950), p. 420, and the interesting paper by Lloyd Street, 'Game Forms in the Factory Group', *Berkeley Publications in Society and Institutions*, 4 (1958), especially pp. 48–50: Piling consisted of passing to the 'speed artist' or 'ratebuster' a greater number of units than he could possibly assemble. The results of the game were to embarrass and ridicule the fast worker without hurting any of the members of the line. Typically it was necessary to pile the 'ratebuster' but once or twice in order to bring him into line with the production norms (p. 48).

It can be argued that informal social participation is an ultimate validation of relationships of intimacy and equality with those with whom one shares this activity.[83] A party, then, is by way of being a status blood bath, a leveling up and leveling down of all present, a mutual contamination and sacralization. Concretely phrased, a party is an opportunity to engage in encounters that will widen one's social horizons through, for example, sexual bond-formation, informality with those of high rank, or extending one's invitation circle. Where boundaries have already been tentatively widened, parties can function to confirm and consolidate work begun elsewhere.

Thus defined, a party presents us with a double set of requirements and, behind these, another illustration of our double theme. On one hand, we can look to the common rationalizations and causes of social endogamy, the ruler that only equals be invited to a sociable gathering. When we ask persons about their exclusiveness, they tend to claim that they would not have 'anything in common' with those not invited and that mixing different classes of persons makes everyone 'uncomfortable'. Presumably, what they mean here is that officially irrelevant attributes would obtrude upon the occasion, destroying the identities upon which the sociability was organized and killing spontaneous involvement in the recreation at hand.

But precisely the opposite concern will be felt, too. Often sociable conversations and games fail not because the participants are insufficiently close socially but because they are not far enough apart. A feeling of boredom, that nothing is likely to happen, can arise when the same persons spend all their sociable moments together. Social horizons cannot be extended. One hears the phrases: 'The same old people', 'the same old thing, let's not go'. The speakers, in fact, usually go, but not hopefully.

So we find that the euphoria function for a sociable occasion resides somewhere between little social difference and much social difference. A dissolution of some externally based social distance must be achieved, a penetration of ego-boundaries, but not to an extent that renders the participants fearful, threatened, or self-consciously

83. This view of sociability derives from W. L. Warner. He seems to have been the first American sociologist to have appreciated and studied this structural role of informal social life. For a recent treatment of sociability that deals with many of the themes discussed in this paper, see D. Riesman, R. J. Potter, and J. Watson, 'Sociability, Permissiveness, and Equality', *Psychiatry*, 23 (1960), pp. 323–40.

concerned with what is happening socially. Too much potential loss and gain must be guarded against, as well as too little.

Too much or too little of this 'working through' will force participants to look directly at the kind of work that parties are expected to do and at the impulses that cause persons to attend or stay away – impulses that ought to be concealed in what is done at parties even while providing the energy for doing it. Sociologically speaking, a very decorous party, as well as an indecorous one, can become obscene, exposing desires out of the context in which they can be clothed by locally realized events.

From this it follows, of course, that what is a successful and happy occasion for one participant may not be such for another. Further, it follows that if the many are to be pleased, then the few may have to sacrifice themselves to the occasion, allowing their bodies to be cast into the blend to make the bell sound sweet. Perhaps they rely at such times on other kinds of pleasures.

CONCLUSIONS

I have argued in this paper that any social encounter, any focused gathering, is to be understood, in the first instance, in terms of the functioning of the 'membrane' that encloses it, cutting it off from a field of properties that could be given weight. There is a set of transformation rules that officially lays down what sorts of properties are to be given what kind of influence in the allocation of locally realized resources. If a participant can become spontaneously involved in the focus of attention prescribed by these transformation rules, he will feel natural, at ease, sure about the reality in which he and the others are sustained. An encounter provides a world for its participants, but the character and stability of this world is intimately related to its selective relationship to the wider one. The naturalistic study of encounters, then, is more closely tied to studies of social structure on one hand, and more separate from them, than one might at first imagine.

I have attempted to show the effects of standard socio-economic attributes on the workings of an encounter. In this, a course has been followed that is customary in sociological analysis, but one important difference must be noted. Empirically, the effect of externally based social attributes on social encounters is very great. But the analysis and theory of this effect must give equal weight to matters such as noise, fatigue, or facial disfigurations. The race-group status of one participant in a focused gathering can have something of the same effect as the harelip of another; the route through which socio-economic factors enter an encounter is one that is equally open to a strange and undignified set of vehicles.

As far as gaming encounters and other focused gatherings are concerned, the most serious thing to consider is the fun in them. Something in which the individual can become unself-consciously engrossed is something that can become real to him. Events that occur in his immediate physical presence are ones in which he can become easily engrossed. *Joint* engrossment in something with others reinforces the reality carved out by the individual's attention, even while subjecting this entrancement to the destructive distractions that the others are now in a position to cause.

The process of mutually sustaining a definition of the situation in face-to-face interaction is socially organized through rules of relevance and irrelevance. These rules for the management of engrossment appear to be an insubstantial element of social life, a matter of courtesy, manners, and etiquette. But it is to these flimsy rules, and not to the unshaking character of the external world, that we owe our unshaking sense of realities. To be at ease in a situation is to be properly subject to these rules, entranced by the meanings they generate and stabilize; to be ill at ease means that one is ungrasped by immediate reality and that one loosens the grasp that others have of it. To be awkward or unkempt, to talk or move wrongly, is to be a dangerous giant, a destroyer of worlds. As every psychotic and comic ought to know, any accurately improper move can poke through the thin sleeve of immediate reality.

ROLE DISTANCE[1]

1. I am grateful to the Center for the Integration of Social Science Theory, of the University of California, Berkeley, and the Society for the Study of Human Ecology, New York, for support during the preparation of this paper. I have profited from criticisms by Aaron Cicourel, John Clausen, Fred Davis, Melvin Kohn, Sheldon Messinger, Theodore Sarbin, David Schneider, and Gregory Stone.

In sociology there are few concepts more commonly used than 'role', few that are accorded more importance, and few that waver so much when looked at closely. In this paper I want to consider a broadened version of role and one of the concepts required to do this systematically.

ROLE CONCEPTS

The classic formulation of role concepts comes from the social-anthropological tradition[2] and has led to the development of a conceptual framework sometimes called 'role theory'. A *status* is a position in some system or pattern of positions and is related to the other positions in the unit through reciprocal ties, through rights and duties binding on the incumbents. *Role* consists of the activity the incumbent would engage in were he to act solely in terms of the normative demands upon someone in his position. Role in this normative sense is to be distinguished from *role performance* or role enactment, which is the actual conduct of a particular individual while on duty in his position. (Accordingly, it is a position that can be entered, filled, and left, not a role, for a role can only be performed; but no student seems to hold to these consistencies, nor will I.) In describing a role there is, of course, a problem of how much detail to give, the amount sometimes being tacitly determined unsystematically by the degree of familiarity the reader is assumed to have with the role in question.

The individual's role enactment occurs largely through a cycle of face-to-face social situations with *role others*, that is, relevant audiences. These various kinds of role others for an individual in role, when taken together, have recently been termed a *role-set*.[3] The role-

2. Principally Ralph Linton, *The Study of Man* (New York: Appleton-Century, 1936), especially ch. 8, 'Status and Rôle'.

3. R. K. Merton, 'The Role-Set: Problems in Sociological Theory', *British Journal of Sociology*, 8 (1957), pp. 106–120. Presumably, a term will be needed to

set for a doctor, for example, contains colleagues, nurses, patients, and hospital administrators. The norms relating the individual to performers of one of the roles in his role-set will have a special and non-conflictful relation to one another – more so than the norms relating the individual to different kinds of role others. The overall role associated with a position falls into *role sectors*[4] or subroles, each having to do with a particular kind of role other. Doctor–nurse is a role sector of the doctor role; doctor–patient, another. Social changes in a role can be traced by the loss or gain to the role-set of types of role other. However, even within the special sector of a role relating the performer to one type of role other, the activities involved may themselves fall into different, somewhat independent parcels or bundles, and through time these may also be reduced or added to, a bundle at a time. In any case, we ought not to be embarrassed by the fact that what is handled from one kind of position in one organization may be apportioned to two or three kinds of positions in another organization. We need only claim to know how a role is likely to be broken up should it come to be divided – the points of cleavage – and what roles are likely to be combined at times of organizational retrenchment.

The elementary unit of role analysis, as Linton was at pains to point out,[5] is not the individual but the individual enacting his bundle of obligatory activity. The system or pattern borrows only a part of the individual, and what he does or is at other times and places is not the first concern. The role others for whom he performs similarly represent only slices of these others. Presumably his contribution and their contribution, differentiated and interdependent, fit together into a single assemblage of activity, this *system* or pattern being the real concern of role analysis.

The role perspective has definite implications of a social-psychological kind. In entering the position, the incumbent finds that he must take on the whole array of action encompassed by the corres-

refer to the complement of individuals within *one* element in the role set, so that we can discuss the fact that some role others, such as wife, contain only one performer, while other role others, such as patient, contain many.

4. Neal Gross, Ward Mason, and Alexander McEachern, *Explorations in Role Analysis* (New York: Wiley, 1958), especially p. 62. This book provides a very useful treatment of role. See also the helpful article by F. L. Bates, 'Position, Role, and Status: A Reformulation of Concepts', *Social Forces*, 34 (1956), pp. 313–21.

5. Linton, op. cit., p. 113.

ponding role, so role implies a social determinism and a doctrine about socialization. We do not take on items of conduct one at a time but rather a whole harness load of them and may anticipatorily learn to be a horse even while being pulled like a wagon.[6] Role, then, is the basic unit of socialization. It is through roles that tasks in society are allocated and arrangements made to enforce their performance.

Recruitment for positions is restrictively regulated in some way, assuring that the incumbents will possess certain minimal qualifications, official and unofficial, technically relevant and irrelevant.[7] Incumbency tends to be symbolized through status cues of dress and manner, permitting those who engage in a situation to know with whom they are dealing. In some cases there will also be a role term of reference and address. Each position tends to be accorded some invidious social value, bringing a corresponding amount of prestige or contamination to the individual who fills it.

For this paper, it is important to note that in performing a role the individual must see to it that the impressions of him that are conveyed in the situation are compatible with role-appropriate personal qualities effectively imputed to him: a judge is supposed to be deliberate and sober; a pilot, in a cockpit, to be cool; a book-keeper to be accurate and neat in doing his work. These personal qualities, effectively imputed and effectively claimed, combine with a position's title, when there is one, to provide a basis of *self-image* for the incumbent and a basis for the image that his role others will have of him. A self, then, virtually awaits the individual entering a position; he need only conform to the pressures on him and he will find a *me* ready-made for him. In the language of Kenneth Burke, doing is being.

Sociologists have added several concepts to round out the Lintonian perspective; these can be introduced here, along with some effort at clarification.

It can be useful to distinguish between the *regular performance* of a role and a *regular performer* of a role. If, for example, a funeral parlor is to stay in business, then the role of the director, of the immediately bereaved, and of the deceased must be performed regularly; but, of these regularly performed roles, only the director will be a regular performer. The immediately bereaved may play the

6. See Orville Brim, unpublished paper, 'Socialization as Role Learning'.
7. E. C. Hughes, 'Dilemmas and Contradictions of Status', *American Journal of Sociology*, 50 (1945), pp. 353–9.

same role on a few other occasions, but certainly the role of the deceased is played but once by any one individual. We can now see that to speak in common-sense terms of an 'irregular' performer is to refer to someone performing only a few times what is usually performed by a regular performer.

The *function* of a role is the part it plays in the maintenance or destruction of the system or pattern as a whole, the terms *eufunction* and *dysfunction* sometimes being employed to distinguish the supportive from the destructive efforts.[8] Where the functional effect of a role is openly known and avowed, the term *manifest* function is sometimes employed; where these effects are not regularly foreseen and, especially, where this foresight might alter effects, the term *latent* is sometimes used.[9]

A concept that is often employed in the discussion of roles is that of *commitment*. I propose to restrict this term to questions of impersonally enforced structural arrangements. An individual becomes committed to something when, because of the fixed and interdependent character of many institutional arrangements, his doing or being this something irrevocably conditions other important possibilities in his life, forcing him to take courses of action, causing other persons to build up their activity on the basis of his continuing in his current undertakings, and rendering him vulnerable to unanticipated consequences of these undertakings.[10] He thus becomes locked into a position and coerced into living up to the promises and sacrifices built into it. Typically, a person will become deeply committed only to a role he regularly performs, and it is left to gallants, one-shot gamblers, and the foolhardy to become committed to a role they do not perform regularly.

The self-image available for anyone entering a particular position is one of which he may become affectively and cognitively enamored,

8. M. J. Levy, Jr, *The Structure of Society* (Princeton University Press, 1952,) pp. 76–9. It sometimes seems to be the hope of so-called functional analysis to transform all role analysis into role-function analysis.

9. R. K. Merton, *Social Theory and Social Structure* (Glencoe: The Free Press, revised editn, 1957), ch. 1, 'Manifest and Latent Functions', pp. 19–84, especially definitions, p. 51.

10. This last point is based on the thorough statement by Philip Selznick, *TVA and the Grass Roots* (Berkeley: University of California Press, 1953), pp. 255–9. A general consideration of the term 'commitment' may be found in Howard S. Becker, 'Notes on the Concept of Commitment', *American Journal of Sociology*, 66 (1960), pp. 32–40.

desiring and expecting to see himself in terms of the enactment of the role and the self-identification emerging from this enactment. I will speak here of the individual becoming *attached* to his position and its role, adding only that in the case of larger social units – groups, not positions – attachment is more likely to have a selfless component.[11] An appreciation can grow up concerning how attached an individual ought properly to be to a particular role, giving rise to the possibility that, compared to this moral norm, a performer may be overattached to his role or alienated from it. For example, it is said that a new capitalist of the seventeenth century in Europe who entered and left an area of trade according to the temporary profit in it was felt by members of crafts and guilds to be sinfully unattached to what he dealt in.[12] Currently, it is felt to be sound mental hygiene for an individual to be attached to the role he performs, especially if he is a committed and regular performer of it. In all this there may be a middle-class bias, with our understanding of attachment coming from the learned professions, where attachment traditionally is great, to the neglect of the many roles that persons play with detachment, shame, or resentment.

In describing individuals' attachment to a role, it is sometimes said that they have committed their self-feelings to it, but in this paper I shall try to restrict the concept of commitment to the forced-consequence sense previously suggested.[13] We will then be able to see that while attachment and commitment are often found together, as virtue doth cover necessity, there may also be discrepancies. Adoption agencies, for example, deal with two kinds of couples, the too fertile and the insufficiently fertile, the first being committed to the parent role without being attached to it, and the second being attached to the role without yet being committed to it.

11. Strictly speaking, while it is possible for an individual to become attached to a position (as when a Queen becomes convinced of the public value of monarchical government), to be attached to a position usually means to be attached to one's own incumbency of it.

12. See, for example, Werner Sombart, *The Jews and Modern Capitalism* (Glencoe: The Free Press, 1951), ch. 7, 'The Growth of a Capitalistic Point of View in Economic Life'.

13. K. T. Erikson, in an interesting paper, 'Patient Role and Social Uncertainty – A Dilemma of the Mentally Ill', *Psychiatry*, 20 (1957), pp. 263–74, suggests a different pairing of terms: 'commitment' to refer to the process by which an individual comes to take a role to heart, and 'validation' to refer to the process by which the community comes to accord a given role to the individual, ratifying his right to perform it.

Although traditional role analysis starts by focusing on the pattern or system arising from the differentiation and integration of roles, a second concern has emerged, related to, but analytically quite different from, the first, with the individual as the central unit. It is a basic assumption of role analysis that each individual will be involved in more than one system or pattern and, therefore, perform more than one role. Each individual will, therefore, have several selves, providing us with the interesting problem of how these selves are related. The model of man according to the initial role perspective is that of a kind of holding company for a set of not relevantly connected roles; it is the concern of the second perspective to find out how the individual runs this holding company.

While manifestly participating in one system of roles, the individual will have some capacity to hold in abeyance his involvement in other patterns, thus sustaining one or more dormant roles that are enacted roles on other occasions. This capacity supports a life cycle, a calendar cycle, and a daily cycle of role enactments; such scheduling implies some jurisdictional agreements as to where and what the individual is to be when. This *role-segregation* may be facilitated by *audience-segregation*, so that those who figure in one of the individual's major role-sets do not figure in another, thereby allowing the individual to possess contradictory qualities. Nevertheless, a person such as a surgeon, who keeps his surgical tools off his kitchen table and his wife off his other table, may someday find himself with the role dilemma of treating another both as a kinsman and as a body. The embarrassment and vacillation characteristic of *role conflict* presumably result. The identification of this kind of trouble is not a limitation of role analysis but one of its main values, for we are led to consider mechanisms for avoiding such conflict or dealing with unavoidable conflict.[14]

Given the role perspective, it is of course possible to have a clinical, historical, or biographical interest, and to be concerned with all the roles performed by a particular concrete individual. Usually, however, role analysis is pitched in terms of the roles of some particular category of persons, such as doctor or female. Often, in addition, concern is narrowed to some sphere of life, such as a formal organization, a social establishment, an occupational group, or a task activity.

14. For example, see S. E. Perry and L. C. Wynne, 'Role Conflict, Role Redefinition, and Social Change in a Clinical Research Organization', *Social Forces*, 38 (1959), pp. 62–5.

It may be added that while these distinctions in focus are easy enough to stipulate, it is apparently much less easy to keep within one focus once it has been selected.[15]

LIMITATIONS OF THE ROLE FRAMEWORK

Although the classic conceptions of position and role can deal adequately with many difficulties, there remain some issues that are less easy to resolve.

For example, if we look more closely at the notion of rights and duties we see that these were not well-chosen terms. Linton seems to have had in mind the normative world and the two general ways in which this world could impinge upon the individual: as *obligation*, in terms of an action of his own that he or others can legitimately demand he perform, and as *expectation*,[16] in terms of an action of others that he or they can legitimately insist upon. But the terms 'rights' and 'duties' carry other meanings. Sometimes these words refer to normative involvements – whether obligation or expectation – that are desired or undesired in themselves, apart from moral considerations.[17] The term 'rights' is especially ambiguous. Sometimes it means an obligation that can be fulfilled by any one of a class of acts, choice within the class being open to the actor, as when an executive finds he is at liberty to wear any one of his seven business suits to work just as long as he wears a business suit. Sometimes it means an obligation or expectation of one's own that one is allowed to forego, out of consideration for the other's distaste for it.

These verbal difficulties can easily be corrected. A more important issue is that while social scientists may formally espouse Linton's normative approach, many of these students, and Linton himself, do not adhere to it in practice. What students have in mind when they refer to position and role is something much broader and more adaptable than Linton's definitions provide.

15. A very useful treatment of these issues can be found in Gross, op. cit., pp. 56–7, under the heading 'situational specifications'.

16. This term has the disadvantage of referring to both statistical and normative understandings; Gross, op. cit., p. 59, suggests the term 'anticipations' be used for the former. See also A. W. Gouldner, *Wildcat Strike* (Yellow Springs, Ohio: Antioch Press, 1954), p. 22.

17. See E. Goffman, 'The Nature of Deference and Demeanor', *American Anthropologist*, 58 (1956), pp. 473–4.

An individual's position, defining position as it tends to be used, is a matter of life chances – the likelihood of his undergoing certain fateful experiences, certain trials, tribulations, and triumphs. His position in some sphere of life is his 'situation' there, in the sense employed by existentialists: the image that he and others come to have of him; the pleasures and anxieties he is likely to experience; the contingencies he meets in face-to-face interaction with others; the relationships he is likely to form; his probable alignment and stand on public issues, leading various kinds of persons in various connections to oppose him or support him. I include also the obligations and expectations that very often come to guide his action relative to specified others,[18] admitting as one usual but not inevitable aspect of the scene that Linton defined as the whole picture.[19] From this starting point we can turn to consider either a role system or the manner in which the individual manages his multiple roles: we can also address ourselves without embarrassment to ways in which these two main aims of role analysis impinge on one another.

Role may now be defined, in this corrected version, as the *typical* response of individuals in a particular position. Typical role must of course be distinguished from the actual role performance of a concrete individual in a given position. Between typical response and actual response we can usually expect some difference, if only because the position of an individual, in the terms now used, will depend somewhat on the varying fact of how he perceives and defines his situation. Where there is a normative framework for a given role, we can expect that the complex forces at play upon individuals in the relevant position will ensure that typical role will depart to some degree from the normative model, despite the tendency in social life to transform what is usually done to what ought to be done. In general, then, a distinction must be made among typical role, the normative aspects of role, and a particular individual's actual role performance.

18. There is an asymmetry in the impingement of these two normative domains. The individual's role, being his response to his position, will presumably be more directly involved in his obligations than in his expectations – in what he ought to do, as opposed to what others ought to do in regard to him. It is, therefore, natural to speak of the normative components of a position but the obligatory components of role.

19. I draw this revision of the term position from Herbert Blumer, in 'Race Prejudice as a Sense of Group Position', *Pacific Sociological Review*, 1 (1958), pp. 3–7.

Another issue must now be considered. Earlier it was suggested that role analysis tends to concern itself with categories of persons and not with individuals as such. This formulation permits a troublesome ambiguity. In many cases, the category selected for study is one that is well established as a category in daily life with a role term and stereotyped image all its own: doctor, priest, housewife. In other cases, the category is one that is created by the student, who sees that a given set of persons can profitably be treated together, even if persons in everyday life have not done so. Typically, when a student uses a traditional category, the first issue is not the category's character as a 'collective representation', but whether – just as with a category fabricated solely for study – it brackets off a set of persons whose common life situation is worth looking at sociologically. I shall use the term *analytical category* to refer to a set of persons classed together for purposes of study, whether or not these persons have theretofore been brought together and categorized by the public at large.

To set up an analytical category, one must establish a defining or name attribute, possession of which leads to inclusion in the category. Once this is done, however, we must be careful to see that an analytical category (or the corresponding defining attribute) only provides us with a means of *discerning* or *disclosing* the social fate common to the members of the category. Categories and attributes *may* determine an allocation of social fate, as well as merely disclose it (although hardly determining what is available for allocation), but this stronger possibility must not be read into the discussion unless specifically mentioned. Traditional role analysis is often ambiguous and confusing on this point. For example, all persons called 'Doctor' in a given hospital may enjoy and suffer a common social fate. Legal claims to the title, however, tell us who will fall within the category, and hence who will receive this fate, but will not tell us why or how this particular fate has come to be allocated to members of this category, nor the part played by the title in this determination. We say, loosely, that legal entitlement to the term of address 'Doctor' determines how the entitled person will be treated, when, in fact, we usually merely mean that if we know how a person is addressed, we will know which of the available modes of treatment will be accorded him

The notion that position is part of a pattern or system must now be reappraised. Some formal organizations, especially ones wholly contained in the physically bounded region of a walled-in social establishment, provide a concrete system of activity that can be used as a contextual point of reference. Even here the system-like properties of the organization cannot be taken for granted; but when we take a wider unit, such as a community or a society, there is no obvious concrete system of activity to point to as the pattern or system in which the position has its place. I suggest that a more atomistic frame of reference must be used – and is in fact used in actual studies. When we study role we study the situation of someone of a particular analytical category, and we usually limit our interest to the situation of this kind of person in a place and time: the home during non-working hours; the factory during working hours; the community during one's lifetime; the school during the academic term. But any identification of these contexts as social systems is surely hazardous, requiring for justification an extensive preliminary study seldom undertaken.

SITUATED ACTIVITY SYSTEMS

An object of this paper is to adapt role concepts for use in close studies of moment-to-moment behavior. At the same time, I do not want to gloss over the fact – already stressed – that the 'system of reference' in role analysis is often vague and shifting. I therefore limit myself to activity that occurs entirely within the walls of single social establishments. This is already a grave limitation. The role of doctor can hardly be considered fully by noting what he does in a particular hospital that employs him; a full treatment must cover his round of work visits in the community and, what is more, the special treatment he is given when not ostensibly involved in medical matters at all – a treatment he facilitates by having a special license plate, a special door plate, a special term of address, and a special title on his official documents.

But even limiting interest to a particular establishment is not enough. We can look at the individual's regular participation in such an establishment as a regular sequence of daily activities: our doctor makes rounds, writes out clinical notes, places calls to his office, has staff conferences, spends time in surgery, has coffee and lunch breaks, and so forth. Some of these activities will bring him into face-to-face interaction with others for the performance of a single joint activity, a somewhat closed, self-compensating, self-terminating circuit of interdependent actions – what might be called a *situated activity system*. The performance of a surgical operation is an example. Illustrations from other spheres of life would be: the playing-through of a game; the execution of one run of a small-group experiment; the giving and getting of a haircut. Such systems of activity are to be distinguished from a task performed wholly by a single person, whether alone or in the presence of others, and from a joint endeavor that is 'multi-situated', in that it is executed by subgroups of persons operating from different rooms. I would like to add that in English it is convenient to allow the context to decide the class–member issue, that is, whether one is referring to a class of like activities and a pattern of similarities, or referring to any occasion, trial, or run during which one complete cycle of phases occurs and provides a single illustration of the class and pattern.

Given any individual's sequence of regular activities in a social establishment, *one* regular activity involving a situated system can be singled out for study, since this provides the student with a context in which he can get as close as he is able to raw conduct. We deal, then, with 'small group' phenomena in a natural setting.

When the runs of a situated system are repeated with any frequency, fairly well-developed *situated roles* seem to emerge: action comes to be divided into manageable bundles, each a set of acts that can be compatibly performed by a single participant. In addition to this role formation, there is a tendency for role differentiation to occur, so that the package of activity that the members of one class of participants perform is different from, though dependent on, the set performed by members of another category. A situated role, then, is a bundle of activities visibly performed before a set of others and visibly meshed into the activity these others perform. These kinds of roles, it may be added, differ from roles in general, not only because they are realized and encompassed in a face-to-face social situation, but also because the pattern of which they are a part can be confidently identified as a concrete self-compensating system.

The part that an individual plays in a situated circuit of activity inevitably expresses something about him, something out of which he and the others fashion an image of him. Often, this will be more than what is conveyed by mere accidents and incidents, and different from what is conveyed by membership in the establishment as such and by location in its ranks and offices. A situated self, then, awaits the individual.

As an initial example of a situated system, I would like to draw on
some brief observations of merry-go-rounds. There are senses in
which any patronized ride on a merry-go-round provides an instance
of a natural and objective social unit, an activity circuit, providing
we follow the ride through its full cycle of activity involving a cohort
of persons, each one getting a ticket and using it up together on
the same ride. As is often the case with situated activity systems,
mechanical operations and administrative purpose provides the basis
of the unit. Yet persons are placed on this floor and something organic
emerges. There is a mutual orientation of the participants and –
within limits, it is true – a meshing together of their activity. As with
any face-to-face interaction, there is much chance for communication
and its feedback through a wide variety of signs, for the damping and
surging of response, and for the emergence of homeostatic-like controls. As soon as the ride gets under way, there is a circulation of
feeling among the participants and an 'involvement contour' may
emerge, with collective shifts in the intensity, quality, and objects of
involvement. Every ride, then, can be fruitfully viewed as an instance
or run of a somewhat closed self-realized system. And this is so even
though we know that this episode of reality is tied in with the day's
activity at the merry-go-round, the state of the amusement park
as a whole, the park season, and the community from which the riders
come, just as we know that, for the man who runs the merry-go-
round, a single ride may appear as a hardly distinguishable part of a
day's work.

Some of the concepts introduced earlier regarding positions and
roles can be applied, *mutatis mutandis*, to situated activity circuits.
Certainly in the case of the merry-go-round there is role differentiation: those who ride; those who watch; and those who run the
machine. Further, a role in such a system does imply an image of self,
even a well-rounded one. For the merry-go-round rider, for example,
the self awaiting is one that entails a child's portion of bravery and
muscular control, a child's portion of manliness, and often a child's
title. So, too, we know that children can become attached to such a
role, since some will scream when finally taken off their horses.
Further, some concepts, such as function, can be applied to a situated
circuit of activity better perhaps than anywhere else, since here at
least we deal with a clear-cut, well-bounded, concrete system.

The application of other role concepts to situated activity systems
must be more carefully considered. To what, for example, can a child

commit himself in becoming a rider? In coming to the amusement park, the child may be foregoing another kind of amusement that day. In paying his dime, he is committing some measure of purchasing power, but even for him perhaps no great amount. And once the machine starts, he may have some commitment to finishing the ride, as a person piloting a plane has a commitment to stay with his task until a landing is made. But, in the main, a rider's commitment is small. He can, for example, easily arrange to take on the role or divest himself of it.

The role of merry-go-round operator might constitute a greater commitment, since this role is not only performed regularly but also is likely to be enacted by a regular performer. In following his present line of work, the operator may well have automatically excluded himself from the recruitment channels leading to other kinds of jobs. The money he can make on the job, further, may be committed to the upkeep of his domestic establishment, and his budget may have been planned on the basis of his continuing to operate the concession. Relative to the individuals who ride his steeds, then, he is committed to his position and locked into it.

But this is a loose way of talking, derived from traditional role analysis. If the operator is employed by the amusement park, then he is committed to performing some job in connection with the organization. Within the organization's formal setting, however, he may, in fact, change his situated role, managing the candy and popcorn concession one day and the merry-go-round the next – and on some days even both. Although these changes entail a radical shift in the tasks he performs and in the intimate system of situated activity in which these tasks fit, he may find little change in his situation in life. Even where he owns the concession and has invested all his money in the merry-go-round, he need not be committed to the role of operator but merely to hiring someone to perform the role whose hire he can afford to pay.

The point about looking at situated activity systems, however, is not that some traditional role concepts can be applied in this situational setting, but that the complexities of concrete conduct can be examined instead of by-passed. Where the social content of a situated system faithfully expresses in miniature the structure of the broader social organization in which it is located, then little change in the traditional role analysis is necessary; situated roles would merely be our means of sampling, say, occupational or institutional roles. But where a discrepancy is found, we would be in a position to show proper respect for it.

THE PROBLEM OF EXPRESSION

With this preliminary review and revision of role concepts, and the introduction of the notion of situated activity systems, we can begin to look at the special concern of this paper, the issue of expression. I must backtrack a little at first, however, before proceeding with expression on merry-go-rounds and other situated systems.

I have already reviewed the assumption that when an individual makes an appearance in a given position, he will be the person that the position allows and obliges him to be and will continue to be this person during role enactment. The performer will attempt to make the expressions that occur consistent with the identity imputed to him; he will feel compelled to control and police the expressions that occur. Performance will, therefore, be able to express identity. But we need only state that doing is being to become aware of apparent exceptions, which, furthermore, arise at different points, each throwing light on a different source of instability in the presumed expressiveness of role.

One issue is that roles may not only be *played* but also *played at*, as when children, stage actors, and other kinds of cutups mimic a role for the avowed purpose of make-believe; here, surely, doing is not being. But this is easy to deal with. A movie star who plays at being a doctor is not in the role of doctor but in the role of actor; and this latter role, we are told, he is likely to take quite seriously. The work of his role is to portray a doctor, but the work is only incidental; his actual role is no more make-believe than that of a real doctor – merely better paid. Part of the confusion here, perhaps, has been that actors do not have a right to keep amateurs from playing at being actors in amateur theatricals, a fact that helps give the whole trade a bad name.

A professional actor differs from a child in the degree of perseverance and perfection the professional must manifest in the role he simulates. Professional and child are similar, however, in making no continued effort to convince any audience that performer and performed character are the same, and they are similarly embarrassed when this over-belief occurs. Both are to be contrasted with actors employed in one version or another of the cloak-and-dagger business.

These desperate performers are caught exactly between illusion and reality, and must lead one audience to accept the role portrait as real, even while assuring another audience that the actor in no way is convincing himself.

Further, under certain rare and colorful circumstances, a man who first appears, say, to be a surgeon, accepting others' acceptance of him in this role, may in fact be a knowing imposter, knowing of radical grounds that others do not know they have for not accepting him. And in addition to this classic kind of misrepresentation, there is the situation in which an individual may, against his will, be temporarily misidentified by others who have accepted the wrong cues regarding him. It is a sad fact that a Negro intern or resident in a predominantly white hospital is likely to acquire experience in telling patients and visitors that he cannot see to minor requests because he is not an attendant.

Whether an individual plays a role or plays at it, we can expect that the mechanics of putting it on will typically expose him as being out of character at certain regular junctures. Thus, while a person may studiously stay *in role* while in the staging area of its performance, he may nonetheless *break role* or go out of role when he thinks that no one or no one important can see him. Even a performer of one of our most splendid roles, such as a surgeon, may allow himself to 'go out of play' – to stare vacantly, pick his nose, or comb his hair, all in a manner unbecoming a surgeon – just before he enters the operating room or just after he leaves it. But again, it is just these expressive incongruities that role analysis allows us to perceive and account for.

Furthermore, students these days are increasingly examining 'role dissensus', in connection with the plurality of cultural and group affiliations which differentially impinge upon persons present in a role to one another.[20] Thus, some surgeons are more alive than others to the opinion of patients, others to the opinion of their colleagues, and still others to the view that the hospital management has of them. Each of these audiences is likely to have a somewhat different view of ideal standards of performance; what is one man's ideal for role performance may to another seem almost an infraction.

I want to add a point that is insufficiently appreciated. Before a set of task-like activities can become an identity-providing role, these

20. For example, Gross, op. cit., and A. W. Gouldner, 'Cosmopolitans and Locals: Toward an Analysis of Latent Social Roles – I', *Administrative Science Quarterly*, 2 (1957), pp. 281–306.

activities must be clothed in a moral performance of some kind. Mere efficient enactment is not enough to provide the identity; activities must be built up socially and made something of. Although this role formation or social capitalization of jobs seems the usual practice in urban life, it is by no means universal. There are, for example, ancient inbred island communities of Britain where kinship and fellow-islander status is so fundamental that a native who is employed in a local shop to sell to members of the community is unlikely to build this work activity into a stance to be taken to customers. Such clerks take the point of view of the other not only in manner, as in the case of urban sellers, but also in spirit, the other in this case being treated not as a customer but as a kinsman, as a neighbor, or as a friend. Often, no variation can be observed in tone or manner as the clerk weaves personal gossipy conversation in amongst the words of advice he offers as to which of the local shops (not just his own) sells which product at the most advantageous price. Here, the richness of communal life entails an impoverishment of the self-defining aspects of occupational roles: required tasks are done, but they are scarcely allowed to form the base for the development of a special loyalty and a special orientation to the world.[21] Here doing is not being. The person who is the salesman has a self, but it is not the self of a salesman. Only the manager of the store will display identification with his role, and even he appreciates that he must not throw himself too much into his calling.

The next issue concerning expression requires a more extended consideration.

Whatever an individual does and however he appears, he knowingly and unknowingly makes information available concerning the attributes that might be imputed to him and hence the categories in which he might be placed. The status symbolism in his 'personal front' provides information about his group and aggregate affiliations; his treatment at the hands of others conveys a conception of

21. Interestingly enough, in such communities there is often an appreciation that traditional bases for defining the self must be put aside and those of urban repute encouraged. In the Shetland Islands, where almost every man can do a surprising range of mechanical, electrical, and construction work, one may observe tacit agreements among islanders to support one of their number as a 'specialist' in a skill, allowing him payment for jobs they might have done themselves. Once these specialists are established by reputation, if not by the volume and constancy of their trade, the islanders point to them with pride as evidence of the modernity of the community.

him; the physical milieu itself conveys implications concerning the identity of those who are in it. Face-to-face situations, it may be added, are ones in which a great variety of sign vehicles become available, whether desired or not, and are, therefore, situations in which much information about oneself can easily become available. Face-to-face situations are, in fact, ideal projective fields that the participant cannot help but structure in a characterizing way, so that conclusions can be drawn about him, correct or incorrect, whether he wants it or not.

It should be appreciated that the information the situation provides about an individual who is in it need not be a direct reflection or extension of the local scene itself. By working on a charity case in a slum dwelling, a physician does not become identified with the status of his client; social dirt does not rub off on him. (The socio-economic attributes of those who make up his office practice, however, present another problem.) Similarly, the tourist does not lose caste in appearing in an unsophisticated peasant milieu; the very presence of natives establishes him as a traveler.

The individual stands in a double relationship to attributes that are, or might be, imputed to him. Some attributes he will feel are rightfully his, others he will not; some he will be pleased and able to accept as part of his self-definition, others he will not.[22] There is some relationship between these two variables – between what is right and what is pleasing – in that the individual often feels that pleasing imputations regarding himself are in addition rightful, and unpleasing imputations are, incidentally, undeserved and illegitimate. But this happy relationship between the two variables does not always hold.

Ordinarily, the information that arises in a social situation concerning one of the participants consistently confirms for him and others a particular conception of himself which is, in addition, one that he is prepared to accept, more or less, as both right and desirable. Here, in fact, we have two basic assumptions of the role perspective – that one accepts as an identification of oneself what one is doing at the time, and that once cues have been conveyed about one's positions, the rest of the information becoming available in the situation confirms these initial cues.

But expressive consistency and acceptability are not always in fact maintained. Information incompatible with the individual's image of

22. Psychiatrically, this is sometimes referred to as a difference between ego-syntonic and ego-alien.

himself does get conveyed. In some cases, this inopportune information may give the individual more credit than he feels he could properly accept; in more cases, apparently, the troublesome information
undercuts the individual's self-image. Some of this self-threatening
information may be valid, referring to facts which the individual
wishes would not be raised concerning him. Some of the information
may be invalid, implying an unwarranted image of himself that he
ought not to have to accept.

In any case, it should be clear that the individual cannot completely control the flow of events in a social situation and hence
cannot completely control the information about himself that becomes available in the situation. Even the best run interactions throw
up events that are expressively somewhat inconsistent with effective
claims regarding self. Men trip, forget names, wear slightly inappropriate clothes, attempt to buy a too-small amount of some commod-
ity, fail to score well in a game, arrive a few minutes late for an
appointment, become a trifle overheated in argument, fail to finish
a task quite on time. In all these cases, a momentary discrepancy
arises between what the individual anticipated being and what events
imply he is.

Whether a social situation goes smoothly or whether expressions
occur that are in discord with a participant's sense of who and what
he is, we might expect – according to the usual deterministic implications of role analysis – that he will fatalistically accept the information that becomes available concerning him. Yet when we get close
to the moment-to-moment conduct of the individual we find that he
does not remain passive in the face of the potential meanings that are
generated regarding him, but, so far as he can, actively participates in
sustaining a definition of the situation that is stable and consistent
with his image of himself.

Perhaps the simplest example of this 'control of implications'
response is the 'explanation'. Here, the individual volunteers information which is designed to alter radically the information that has been,
or otherwise will be, generated in the situation. Another is that of the
'apology', through which the individual begs not to be judged in
the way that appears likely, implying that his own standards are
offended by his act and that therefore some part of him, at least, cannot be characterized by the unseemly action.[23] A display of righteous

23. Explanations and apologies are, of course, often combined into the 'excuse'
through which both restructuring information and self-abasement are introduced

indignation has the same effect, but it is the other who is cast in a bad light instead of a split-off portion of oneself. Similarly, by introducing an unserious style, the individual can project the claim that nothing happening at the moment to him or through him should be taken as a direct reflection of him, but rather of the person-in-situation that he is mimicking. Thus, there is in our society a special tone of voice and facial posture through which 'baby talk' is conveyed at strategic moments, for example when a second helping is requested by an individual who does not want to appear to be intemperate.

Explanations, apologies, and joking are all ways in which the individual makes a plea for disqualifying some of the expressive features of the situation as sources of definitions of himself. Since these maneuvers are often accepted by the others present, we must see that the individual's responsibility for the self-expressive implications of the events around him has definite limits.

ROLE DISTANCE

The occurrence of explanations and apologies as limitations on the expressiveness of role leads us to look again at what goes on in concrete face-to-face activity. I return to our situated example, the merry-go-round.

A merry-go-round horse is a thing of some size, some height, and some movement; and while the track is never wet, it can be very noisy. American middle-class two-year-olds often find the prospect too much for them. They fight their parents at the last moment to avoid being strapped into a context in which it had been hoped they would prove to be little men. Sometimes they become frantic halfway through the ride, and the machine must be stopped so that they can be removed.

Here we have one of the classic possibilities of life. Participation in any circuit of face-to-face activity requires the participant to keep command of himself, both as a person capable of executing physical movements and as one capable of receiving and transmitting communications. A flustered failure to maintain either kind of role poise makes the system as a whole suffer. Every participant, therefore, has the function of maintaining his own poise, and one or more partici-

at the same time. See the treatment in Jackson Toby, 'Some Variables in Role Conflict Analysis', *Social Forces*, 30 (1952), pp. 323–37.

pants are likely to have the specialized function of modulating activity so as to safeguard the poise of the others. In many situated systems, of course, all contingencies are managed without such threats arising. However, there is no such system in which these troubles might not occur, and some systems, such as those in a surgery ward, presumably provide an especially good opportunity to study these contingencies.

Just as a rider may be disqualified during the ride because he proves to be unable to handle riding, so a rider will be removed from his saddle at the very beginning of the ride because he does not have a ticket or because, in the absence of his parents, he makes management fear for his safety. There is an obvious distinction, then, between qualifications required for permission to attempt a role and attributes required for performing suitably once the role has been acquired.

At three and four, the task of riding a wooden horse is still a challenge, but apparently a manageable one, inflating the rider to his full extent with demonstrations of capacity. Parents need no longer ride alongside to protect their youngsters. The rider throws himself into the role in a serious way, playing it with verve and an admitted engagement of all his faculties. Passing his parents at each turn, the rider carefully lets go one of his hands and grimly waves a smile or a kiss – this, incidentally, being an example of an act that is a typical part of the role but hardly an obligatory feature of it. Here, then, doing is being, and what was designated as a 'playing at' is stamped with serious realization.

Just as 'flustering' is a classic possibility in all situated systems, so also is the earnest way these youngsters of three or four ride their horses. Three matters seem to be involved: an admitted or expressed attachment to the role; a demonstration of qualifications and capacities for performing it; an active *engagement* or spontaneous involvement in the role activity at hand, that is, a visible investment of attention and muscular effort. Where these three features are present, I will use the term *embracement*. To embrace a role is to disappear completely into the virtual self available in the situation, to be fully seen in terms of the image, and to confirm expressively one's acceptance of it. To embrace a role is to be embraced by it. Particularly good illustrations of full embracement can be seen in persons in certain occupations: team managers during baseball games; traffic policemen at intersections during rush hours; landing signal officers who wave in planes landing on the decks of aircraft carriers; in fact, any one occupying a directing role where the performer must guide others by means of gestural signs.[24]

An individual may affect the embracing of a role in order to conceal a lack of attachment to it, just as he may affect a visible disdain for a role, thrice refusing the kingly crown, in order to defend himself against the psychological dangers of his actual attachment to it. Certainly an individual may be attached to a role and fail to be able to embrace it, as when a child proves to have no ticket or to be unable to hang on.

Returning to the merry-go-round, we see that at five years of age the situation is transformed, especially for boys. To be a merry-go-round horse rider is now apparently not enough, and this fact must be demonstrated out of dutiful regard for one's own character. Parents are not likely to be allowed to ride along, and the strap for preventing falls is often disdained. One rider may keep time to the music by clapping his feet or a hand against the horse, an early sign of utter control. Another may make a wary stab at standing on the saddle or changing horses without touching the platform. Still another may hold on to the post with one hand and lean back as far as possible while looking up to the sky in a challenge to dizziness. Irreverence begins, and the horse may be held on to by his wooden ear or his tail. The child says by his actions: 'Whatever I am, I'm not just someone who can barely manage to stay on a wooden horse.' Note that what the rider is apologizing for is not some minor untoward event that has cropped up during the interaction, but the whole role. The image of him that is generated for him by the routine entailed in his mere participation – his virtual self in the context – is an image from which he apparently withdraws by *actively* manipulating the situation. Whether this skittish behavior is intentional or unintentional, sincere or affected, correctly appreciated by others present or not, it does constitute a wedge between the individual and his role, between doing and being. This 'effectively' expressed pointed separateness between the individual and his putative role I shall call *role distance*. A shorthand is involved here: the individual is actually denying not the role but the virtual self that is implied in the role for all accepting performers.

In any case, the term 'role distance' is not meant to refer to all behavior that does not directly contribute to the task core of a given role but only to those behaviors that are seen by someone present as

24. Here, as elsewhere, I am indebted to Gregory Stone.

relevant to assessing the actor's attachment to his particular role and relevant in such a way as to suggest that the actor possibly has some measure of disaffection from, and resistance against, the role. Thus, for example, a four-year-old halfway through a triumphant performance as a merry-go-round rider may sometimes go out of play, dropping from his face and manner any confirmation of his virtual self, yet may indulge in this break in role without apparent intent, the lapse reflecting more on his capacity to sustain any role than on his feelings about the present one. Nor can it be called role distance if the child rebels and totally rejects the role, stomping off in a huff, for the special facts about self that can be conveyed by holding a role off a little are precisely the ones that cannot be conveyed by throwing the role over.

At seven and eight, the child not only dissociates himself self-consciously from the kind of horseman a merry-go-round allows him to be but also finds that many of the devices that younger people use for this are now beneath him. He rides no-hands, gleefully chooses a tiger or a frog for a steed, clasps hands with a mounted friend across the aisle. He tests limits, and his antics may bring negative sanction from the adult in charge of the machine. And he is still young enough to show distance by handling the task with bored, nonchalant competence, a candy bar languidly held in one hand.

At eleven and twelve, maleness for boys has become a real responsibility, and no easy means of role distance seems to be available on merry-go-rounds. It is necessary to stay away or to exert creative acts of distancy, as when a boy jokingly treats his wooden horse as if it were a racing one: he jogs himself up and down, leans far over the neck of the horse, drives his heels mercilessly into its flanks, and uses the reins for a lash to get more speed, brutally reining in the horse when the ride is over. He is just old enough to achieve role distance by defining the whole undertaking as a lark, a situation for mockery.

Adults who choose to ride a merry-go-round display adult techniques of role distance. One adult rider makes a joke of tightening the safety belt around him; another crosses his arms, giving popcorn with his left hand to the person on his right and a coke with his right hand to the person on his left. A young lady riding sidesaddle tinkles out, 'It's cold,' and calls to her watching boy friend's boy friend, 'Come on, don't be chicken.' A dating couple riding adjacent horses hold hands to bring sentiment, not daring, to the situation. Two double-dating couples employ their own techniques: the male in front sits backwards and takes a picture of the other male rider taking a picture of him. And, of course, some adults, riding close by their threatened two-and-a-half-year-old, wear a face that carefully demonstrates that they do not perceive the ride as an event in itself, their only present interest being their child.

And finally there is the adult who runs the machine and takes the tickets. Here, often, can be found a fine flowering of role distance. Not only does he show that the ride itself is not – as a ride – an event to him, but he also gets off and on and around the moving platform with a grace and ease that can only be displayed by safely taking what for children and even adults would be chances.

Some general points can be made about merry-go-round role distance. First, while the management of a merry-go-round horse in our culture soon ceases to be a challenging 'developmental task', the task of expressing that it is not continues for a long time to be a challenge and remains a felt necessity. A full twist must be made in the iron law of etiquette: the act through which one can afford to try to fit into the situation is an act that can be styled to show that one is somewhat out of place. One enters the situation to the degree that one can demonstrate that one does not belong.

A second general point about role distance is that immediate audiences figure very directly in the display of role distance. Merry-go-round horsemen are very ingenuous and may frankly wait for each time they pass their waiting friends before playing through their gestures of role distance. Moreover, if persons above the age of twelve or so are to trust themselves to making a lark of it, they almost need to have a friend along on the next horse, since persons who are 'together' seem to be able to hold off the socially defining force of the environment much more than a person alone.

A final point: two different means of establishing role distance seem to be found. In one case the individual tries to isolate himself as much as possible from the contamination of the situation, as when an adult riding along to guard his child makes an effort to be completely stiff, affectless, and preoccupied. In the other case the individual cooperatively projects a childish self, meeting the situation more than half-way, but then withdraws from this castoff self by a little gesture signifying that the joking has gone far enough. In either case the individual can slip the skin the situation would clothe him in.

A summary of concepts is now in order. I have tried to distinguish among three easily confused ideas: *commitment*, *attachment*, and *embracement*.[25] It is to be noted that these sociological terms are of a different order from that of *engagement*, a psychobiological process that a cat or a dog can display more beautifully than man. Finally, the term *role distance* was introduced to refer to actions which effectively convey some disdainful detachment of the performer from a role he is performing.

ROLE DISTANCE AND SERIOUS ACTIVITY

The role of merry-go-round rider can be regularly performed at any amusement park but hardly by a regular performer. After a few years each of us 'outgrows' the role and can only perform it as an occasional thing and as an occasion for the display of much role distance. As an example, then, merry-go-round riding is not a very serious one; furthermore, it is somewhat misleading, since it implies that role distance is displayed in connection with roles no adult can take seriously.

Actually, we deal with a more general phenomenon, with roles that categories of individuals find it unwise to embrace. Even a short step away from merry-go-rounds show this. Take, for example, six lower-middle-class high-schools girls, not of the horsy set, taking a vacation in a national park and deciding to 'do' horseback riding on one of their mornings. As long as they come to the riding stable in self-supporting numbers, they can nicely illustrate distance from a role that persons of another social class and region might take seriously all their lives. The six I observed came in clothing patently not designed as a consolidation of the horsewoman role: pedal pushers, cotton leotards, ballet-type flats, frilly blouses. One girl, having been allotted the tallest horse, made a mock scene of declining to get on because of the height, demanding to be allowed to go home. When she did get on, she called her horse 'Daddy-O', diverting her conversation from her friends to her horse. During the ride, one girl pretended to post while the horse walked, partly in mockery of a person not in their party who was posting. Another girl leaned over the neck of her horse and shouted racing cries, again while the horse was locked in a walking file of other horses. She also slipped her right foot out of the stirrup and

25. A somewhat different and more differentiated analysis may be found in G. P. Stone, 'Clothing and Social Relations: A Study of Appearance in the Context of Community Life' (unpublished Ph.D. dissertation, Department of Sociology, University of Chicago, 1959).

brought it over the saddle, making a joke of her affectation of riding sidesaddle and expressing that both positions were much alike to her – both equally unfamiliar and uncongenial; at the same time she tested the limits of the wrangler's permissiveness. Passing under low branches, the girls made a point of making a point of this by pulling off branches, waving them like flags, then feeding them to their horses. Evidences of the excretory capacities of the steeds were greeted with merriment and loud respect. During the latter part of the two-hour ride, two of the girls became visibly bored, dropped the reins over the saddlehorn, let their hands fall limply to their sides, and gave up all pretense at being in role.

Again we can detect some general facts about role distance. We can see that a role that some persons take seriously most of their lives may be one that others will never take seriously at any age. We see that participation with a group of one's similars can lead strength to the show of role distance and to one's willingness to express it. In the presence of age-peers elegantly attired for riding and skilled at it, the girls I observed might falter in displaying role distance, feeling hostile, resentful, and unconfident. Presumably, if one of these girls were alone with thoroughgoing horsewomen she would be even less prone to flourish this kind of distance. We can suspect, then, that role distance will have defensive functions. By manifesting role distance, the girls give themselves some elbow room in which to maneuver. 'We are not to be judged by this incompetence,' they say. Should they make a bad showing, they are in a position to dodge the reflection it could cast on them. Whatever their showing, they avoid having to be humbled before those who are socially placed to make a much better showing. By exposing themselves in a guise to which they have no serious claim, they leave themselves in full control of shortcomings they take seriously.

While horse trails and children's playgrounds provide fine places for studying repertoires of role distance, we need not look to situations that are so close to being unserious, situations where it is difficult to distinguish role playing from playing at. We know, for example, that tasks that might be embraced by a housewife or maid may be tackled by the man of the house with carefully expressed clumsiness and with self-mockery. Perhaps it should be noted that similar out-of-character situations can easily be created experimentally by asking subjects to perform tasks that are inappropriate to persons of their kind.

The published literature on some of our occupational byways provides serious material on role distance. Psychoanalysts, for example, who have told us so much about the contingencies of a particular trade (even when not telling us all we might want to know about their patients), provide interesting data on role distance in connection with 'resistance' on the part of the patient. Resistance here takes the form of the patient refusing to provide relevant associations or refusing to allow the therapist to function solely as a 'therapist'. From the therapist's view of the patient's motivation, then, resistance expresses some rejection of the constraints of one's role as patient:

Up to this point I found myself, as the doctor, comfortably installed in my explicit instrumental role; the role assignment given me by the patient appeared to be concerned with her 'problem'. The system of roles was complementary and apparently well integrated. The next moment, however, the patient initiated a new role assignment. She asked me if I had seen a recent performance of 'Don Juan in Hell' from *Man and Superman*. The question seemed a simple enough request for information regarding my playgoing habits. But since I did not know what role I was being invited to take, and because I suspected that behind whatever explicit role this might turn out to be there lurked a more important implicit one, I did not answer the question. The patient paused for a moment, and then, perceiving that I would not answer the question, she continued . . .

In continuing after the pause, the patient delivered a highly perceptive account of Shaw's intention in the Don Juan interlude, of the actors' interpretations, and of her reactions. The account was so long that I finally interrupted to ask if she knew why she wanted to tell all this. At the point of interruption I had become aware that my new role was an expressive one – to play the appreciative audience to her role as a gifted art and drama critic.[26]

The therapist then goes on to explain that had he merely fallen in with the patient's maneuver to keep herself at a distance from the role of patient he would have had to pass up 'the opportunity to get more information regarding the hidden, implicit role buried in this transaction and thus to learn more about her motivation for shifting out of her initial instrumental role in which she had started the interview'.[27] The therapist could have added that to ask the patient why she felt it necessary to run on so is a classic therapist's ploy to put the patient in her place, back in role.

26. J. P. Spiegel, 'The Social Roles of Doctor and Patient in Psychoanalysis and Psychotherapy', *Psychiatry*, 17 (1954), pp. 372–3.
27. ibid., p. 373.

Situated roles that place an individual in an occupational setting he feels is beneath him are bound to give rise to much role distance. A good example is provided by Isaac Rosenfeld in a reminiscence about a summer job as a barker at Coney Island. The writer begins his description by telling of his return after many years, seeing someone else handling his old job:

He was sneering, just as I used to do in the old days, and no doubt for the same reason: because the summer was hot, and the work hard, sweaty and irritating, stretching over long hours for poor pay. It was absolutely indispensable, now as it was then, to separate oneself from the job – one had to have a little ledge to stand on all to himself; otherwise perish. I used to pitch this ledge very high. The higher I stood, the greater my contempt, and the more precious the moments of freedom I won for myself by this trick of balancing above the crowd. I remembered how I used to mix T. S. Eliot with my spiel (in those days there was hardly anyone in Freshman English who did not know a good deal of *The Waste Land* by heart): 'Step right up ladies and gentlemen mingling memory with desire for the greatest thrill show on earth only a dime the tenth part of a dollar will bring you to Carthage then I come burning burning burning O Lord thou pluckest me out ten cents!'[28]

Some of the most appealing data on role distance come from situations where a subordinate must take orders or suggestions and must go along with the situation as defined by superordinates. At such times, we often find that although the subordinate is careful not to threaten those who are, in a sense, in charge of the situation, he may be just as careful to inject some expression to show, for any who care to see, that he is not capitulating completely to the work arrangement in which he finds himself.[29] Sullenness, muttering, irony, joking, and sarcasm may all allow one to show that something of oneself lies outside the constraints of the moment and outside the role within whose jurisdiction the moment occurs.

Given these various examples of role distance, I want to go on to argue that this conduct is something that falls between role obliga-

28. Isaac Rosenfeld, 'Coney Island Revisited', in *Modern Writing*, ed. William Phillips and Philip Rahv (New York: Avon Publications, 1953), p. 219.

29. Some excellent illustrations of this may be found in Tom Burns, 'Friends, Enemies and the Polite Fiction', *American Sociological Review*, 18 (1953), pp. 654–62, a paper to which I am very much indebted. A good illustration from army life is provided in William Styron's story, *The Long March* (New York: Modern Library, 1952), in connection with a captain's minor remonstrances against orders issued by his colonel.

tions on one hand and actual role performance on the other. This gap has always caused trouble for sociologists. Often, they try to ignore it. Faced with it, they sometimes despair and turn from their own direction of analysis; they look to the biography of the performer and try to find in his history some particularistic explanation of events, or they rely on psychology, alluding to the fact that in addition to playing the formal themes of his role, the individual always behaves personally and spontaneously, phrasing the standard obligations in a way that has a special psychological fit for him.

The concept of role distance provides a *sociological* means of dealing with one type of divergence between obligation and actual performance. First, we know that often distance is not introduced on an individual basis but can be predicted on the grounds of the performers' gross age-sex characteristics. Role distance is a part (but, of course, only one part) of *typical* role, and this routinized sociological feature should not escape us merely because role distance is not part of the normative framework of role. Secondly, that which one is careful to point out one is not, or not merely, necessarily has a directing and intimate influence on one's conduct, especially since the means for expressing this disaffection must be carved out of the standard materials available in the situation.

We arrive, then, at a broadened sociological way of looking at the trappings of a social role. A set of visible qualifications and known certifications, along with a social setting well designed as a showplace, provides the individual with something more than an opportunity to play his role self to the hilt, for this scene is just what he needs to create a clear impression of what he chooses not to lay claim to. The more extensive the trappings of a role, the more opportunity to display role distance. Personal front and social setting provide precisely the field an individual needs to cut a figure in – a figure that romps, sulks, glides, or is indifferent. Later in this paper, some additional social determinants of role distance will be considered.

SURGERY AS AN ACTIVITY SYSTEM

I have suggested some cases where the scene of activity generates for the individual a self which he is apparently loath to accept openly for himself, since his conduct suggests that some disaffiliation exists between himself and his role. But a peek into some odd corners of social life provides no basis, perhaps, for generalizing about social life. As a test, then, of the notion of role distance (and role), let us take a scene in which activity generates a self for the individual that appears to be a most likely one for self-attachment. Let us take, for example, the activity system sustained during a surgical operation. The components consist of verbal and physical acts and the changing state of the organism undergoing the operation. Here, if anywhere in our society, we should find performers flushed with a feeling of the weight and dignity of their action. A Hollywood ideal is involved: the white-coated chief surgeon strides into the operating theater after the patient has been anesthetized and opened by assistants. A place is automatically made for him. He grunts a few abbreviated preliminaries, then deftly, almost silently, gets to work, serious, grim, competently living up to the image he and his team have of him, yet in a context where momentary failure to exhibit competence might permanently jeopardize the relation he is allowed to have to his role. Once the critical phase of the operation is quite over, he steps back and, with a special compound of tiredness, strength, and disdain, rips off his gloves; he thus contaminates himself and abdicates his role, but at a time when his own labors put the others in a position to 'close up'. While he may be a father, a husband, or a baseball fan at home, he is here one and only one thing, a surgeon, and being a surgeon provides a fully rounded impression of the man. If the role perspective works, then, surely it works here, for in our society the surgeon, if anyone, is allowed and obliged to put himself into his work and get a self out of it.[30]

As a contrast, then, to the insubstantial life of horses-for-ride, I want to report briefly on some observations of activity in surgery wards.[31]

30. Much the same conceit has already been employed by Temple Burling in *Essays on Human Aspects of Administration*, Bulletin 25 (August, 1953) of the New York State School of Industrial and Labor Relations, Cornell University, pp. 9–10. The fullest published accounts of conduct in the operating room that I know of are to be found in T. Burling, E. Lentz and R. Wilson, *The Give and Take in Hospitals* (New York: Putnam, 1956), ch. 17, pp. 260–83, and R. Wilson, 'Teamwork in the Operating Room', *Human Organization*, 12 (1954), pp. 9–14.

31. My own material on interaction during surgery, from which all staff practices and verbal responses cited in this paper are drawn, derives from brief observations in the medical building of a mental hospital and the operating rooms of a suburban community hospital. Not deriving from the most formal hospitals, these data load the facts a little in my favor.

I am grateful to Dr Otis R. Farley, and his staff in the Medical and Surgical

If we start with the situation of the lesser medical personnel, the intern and the junior resident, the test will not be fair, for here, apparently, is a situation much like the ones previously mentioned. The tasks these juniors are given to do – such as passing hemostats, holding retractors, cutting small tied-off veins, swabbing the operating area before the operation, and perhaps suturing or closing at the end – are not large enough to support much of a surgical role. Furthermore, the junior person may find that he performs even these lowly tasks inadequately, and that the scrub nurse as well as the chief surgeon tells him so. And when the drama is over and the star performer has dropped his gloves and gown and walked out, the nurses may underline the intern's marginal position by lightly demanding his help in moving the body from the fixed table to the movable one, while automatically granting him a taste of the atmosphere they maintain when real doctors are absent. As for the intern himself, surgery is very likely *not* to be his chosen specialty; the three-month internship is a course requirement and he will shortly see the last of it. The intern may confirm all this ambivalence to his work on occasions away from the surgery floor, when he scathingly describes surgery as a plumber's craft exercised by mechanics who are told what to look for by internists.

The surgical junior, especially the intern, has, then, a humbling position during surgery. Whether as a protection against this condition or not, the medical juniors I observed, like over-age merry-go-round riders, analysands, and carnival pitchmen, were not prepared to embrace their role fully; elaborate displays of role distance occurred.[32] A careful, bemused look on the face is sometimes found, implying, 'This is not the real me.' Sometimes the individual will allow himself to go 'away', dropping off into a brown study that removes him from the continuity of events, increases the likelihood that his next contributory act will not quite fit into the flow of action, and effectively gives the appearance of occupational disaffection;

Branch of St Elizabeths Hospital, Washington, D.C., and to John F. Wight, Administrative Director, and Lenore Jones, Head Surgical Nurse, of Herrick Memorial Hospital, Berkeley, California, for full research freedom and great courtesy.

32. Some of the interns I observed had plans to take a psychiatric residency and, apparently because of this, were doing their stint of surgical internship in the medical building of a mental hospital; they therefore had wider institutional support for their lack of interest in physical techniques.

brought back into play, he may be careful to evince little sign of chagrin. He may rest himself by leaning on the patient or by putting a foot on an inverted bucket but in a manner too contrived to allow the others to feel it is a matter of mere resting. Interestingly enough, he sometimes takes on the function of the jester, endangering his reputation with antics that temporarily place him in a doubtful and special position, yet through this providing the others present with a reminder of less exalted worlds:

CHIEF SURGEON JONES [*in this case a senior resident*]: A small Richardson please.
SCRUB NURSE: Don't have one.
DR JONES: O.K., then give me an Army and Navy.
SCRUB NURSE: It looks like we don't have one.
DR JONES [*lightly joking*]: No Army or Navy man here.
INTERN [*dryly*]: No one in the armed forces, but Dr Jones here is in the Boy Scouts.

SCRUB NURSE: Will there be more than three [sutures] more? We're running out of sutures.
CHIEF SURGEON: I don't know.
INTERN: We can finish up with Scotch tape.

INTERN [*looking for towel clamps around body*]: Where in the world . . . ?
SCRUB NURSE: Underneath the towel.
    [*Intern turns to the nurse and in slow measure makes a full cold bow to her.*]

SCRUB NURSE (*to intern*): Watch it, you're close to my table! [*A Mayo stand containing instruments whose asepsis she must guard and guarantee.*]
    [*Intern performs a mock gasp and clownishly draws back.*]

As I have suggested, just as we cannot use a child over four riding a merry-go-round as an exhibition of how to embrace an activity role, so also we cannot use the junior medical people on a surgical team. But surely the chief surgeon, at least, will demonstrate the embracing of a role. What we find, of course, is that even this central figure expresses considerable role distance.

Some examples may be cited. One can be found in medical etiquette. This body of custom requires that the surgeon, on leaving the operation, turn and thank his assistant, his anesthetist, and ordinarily his nurses as well. Where a team has worked together for a long time and where the members are of the same age-grade, the surgeon may guy this act, issuing the thanks in what he expects will be taken as an ironical and farcical tone of voice: 'Miss Westly, you've done a simply wonderful job here.' Similarly, there is a formal rule that in preparing a requested injection the nurse show the shelved vial to the surgeon before its sealed top is cracked off so that he can check its named contents and thereby take the responsibility on himself. If the surgeons are very busy at the time, this checking may be requested but not given. At other times, however, the checking may be guyed.

CIRCULATING NURSE: Dr James, would you check this?
DR JAMES [*in a loud ministerial voice, reading the label*]: Three cubic centimeters of heparin at ten-milligram strength, put up by Invenex and held by Nurse Jackson at a forty-five-degree angle. That is right, Nurse Jackson.

Instead of employing technical terms at all times, he may tease the nurses by using homey appellations: 'Give me the small knife, we'll get in just below the belly button'; and he may call the electric cauterizer by the apt name of 'sizzler', ordering the assistant surgeon to 'sizzle here, and here'. Similarly, when a nurse allows her non-sterile undergown to be exposed a little, a surgeon may say in a pontifical and formal tone, 'Nurse Bevan, can I call your attention to the anterior portion of your gown. It is exposing you. I trust you will correct this condition,' thereby instituting social control, reference to the nurse's non-nursing attributes, and satire of the profession, all with one stroke. So, too, a nurse, returning to the operating room with a question, 'Dr Williams?' may be answered by a phrase of self-satirization: 'In person,' or, 'This is Dr Williams.' And a well-qualified surgeon, in taking the situated role of assistant surgeon for the duration of a particular operation, may tell the nurses, when they have been informed by the chief surgeon that two electric cauterizers will be employed, 'I'm going to get one too, just like the big doctors, that's what I like to hear.' A chief surgeon, then, may certainly express role distance. Why he does so, and with what effect, are clearly additional questions, and ought to be considered.

THE FUNCTIONS OF ROLE DISTANCE FOR SURGERY

I have suggested that in surgery, in a room that pridefully keeps out germs and gives equal medical treatment to bodies of different socio-economic status, there is no pretence at expressional asepsis. Role distance is routinely expressed.

But why should the individual be disinclined to embrace his role self? The situation of the junior medical man suggests that defensive activity is at work. We cannot say, however, that role distance protects the individual's ego, self-esteem, personality, or integrity from the implications of the situation without introducing constructs which have no place in a strictly sustained role perspective. We must find a way, then, of getting the ego back into society.

We can begin to do this by noting that when the individual withdraws from a situated self he does not draw into some psychological world that he creates himself but rather acts in the name of some other socially created identity. The liberty he takes in regard to a situated self is taken because of other, equally social, constraints. A first example of this is provided us when we try to obtain a systematic view of the functions performed by role distance in surgery, for immediately we see a paradoxical fact: one of the concerns that prevents the individual from fully accepting his situated self is his commitment to the situated activity system itself. We see this when we shift our point of view from the individual to the situated system and look at the functions that role distance serves for it. We find that certain maneuvers which act to integrate the system require for their execution individuals who do not fully embrace their situated selves. System-irrelevant roles can thus themselves be exploited for the system as a whole. In other words, one of the claims upon himself that the individual must balance against all others is the claim created by the over-all 'needs'[33] of the situated activity system itself, apart from his particular role in it.

An illustration of these contingencies is provided by the chief surgeon. Like those in many other occupational positions, the chief surgeon finds that he has the obligation to direct and manage a particular activity system, in this case a surgical operation. He is obliged to see that the operation is effectively carried through, regardless of what this may sometimes express about himself.

Now for the surgical team to function usefully, each member, as already suggested, must sustain his capacity as a communicator, an individual capable of giving and receiving verbal communications and their substitutes. And, as in other activity systems, each member must be able to execute physical actions requiring some coolness and self-command. Anything that threatens either this verbal or physical

33. In the sense used by Philip Selznick in 'Foundations of the Theory of Organization', *American Sociological Review*, 13 (1948), pp. 29–30.

poise threatens the participant's capacity to contribute, and hence the activity system itself. Each individual member of the surgical team must be in command of himself, and where he is not able to handle himself, others, especially the chief surgeon, must help him to do it.

In order to ensure that the members of his team keep their heads during the operation, the chief surgeon finds himself under pressure to modulate his own demands and his own expectations of what is due to him. If he exercises his situated rights openly to criticize incompetent conduct, the surgeon may only further weaken the defaulter's self-command and further endanger the particular operation. In short, the chief surgeon is likely to find himself with the situated role function of anxiety management[34] and may find that he must draw on his own dignity, on what is owed his station, in order to fulfil this function. A kind of bargaining or bribery[35] occurs, whereby the surgeon receives a guarantee of equability from his team in return for being 'a nice guy' – someone who does not press his rightful claims too far. Of course, the surgeon may save his dignity and lose the operation, but he is under pressure not to do so.

Given the conflict between correcting a subordinate and helping him maintain his poise, it is understandable that surgeons will employ joking means of negative sanction, so that it is difficult to determine whether the joke is a cover for the sanction, or the sanction a cover for the joke. In either case, some distance from usual surgical decorum is required:

> [*Intern holds retractor at wrong end of incision and goes 'away', being uninterested in the operation.*]

CHIEF SURGEON [*in mock English accent*]: You don't have to hold that up there, old chap, perhaps down here. Going to sleep, old boy?

CHIEF SURGEON [*on being accidentally stabbed in the finger by the assistant surgeon, who is using the electric scalpel*]: If I get syphalis [*sic*] I'll know where I got it from, and I'll have witnesses.

If some of these jokes seem weak and unnecessary, we must appreciate that to let a small error of conduct go by without comment has its own dangers, apart from what this laxness might mean for staff training. In the presence of a mistake, staff members can ready them-

34. This role function is one which the M.D. anesthetist often performs, or tries to perform, sometimes apparently quite intentionally, as a filler for a position that might otherwise not have enough weight for the person who fills it.

35. The notion of 'role bargain' is usefully developed in W. J. Goode, 'A Theory of Role Strain', *American Sociological Review*, 25 (1960), pp. 483–96.

selves for the occurrence of a corrective sanction, and unless something pertinent is said, this readiness may act as an anxiety-producing distraction. The immediate expression of a joking sanction, however labored, grounds this source of tension.

Just as a negative sanction may be toned down to prevent the offender from acting still more disruptively, so also direct commands may be softened into requests even though the surgeon's general occupational status and particular situated role empower him to command. Where he has a right to issue a peremptory order for an instrument, he may instead employ courtesies: 'Let's have another Richardson,' 'Could I have a larger retractor?' Instead of flaring up when no suitable ready-made instrument is available, he may choose to express a boyish mechanical ingenuity, constructing on the spot a make-do instrument.[36]

I am suggesting that he who would effectively direct an operation at times may have to employ a touch so light as to embarrass the dark dignities of his position. In fact, we can expect that the more that is demanded from a subordinate in the way of delicacy, skill, and pure concentration, the more informal and friendly the superordinate is likely to become. If one person is to participate in a task as if he were an extension of another participant, opening himself up to the rapid

36. In some face-to-face activity systems a participant may be so close to losing poise that a responsible other may have to modify his whole manner, not merely his commands and negative sanctions, if the unreliable participant is to be kept on his feet, and this modification is likely to be at the expense of formal behavior patterns associated with the superordinate's role. To prevent the full weight of his role from frightening or freezing subordinates, the superordinate may therefore employ informalities. The official who asks an interviewee to join him in a cigarette provides the classic example, known as 'putting a subordinate at his ease'. The strategy employed by a child analyst provides another illustration:

'It is so desirable for the psychoanalyst to remain on the less active side with the child patient that for her to knit is often a good device. The knitting should be on something for the patient so that he will not feel that the busy-work takes away from him. The knitting serves to occupy the therapist who may have an inclination to play with the child or the need to press the child into some significant productions. It also serves to modify the seductiveness of the analytical experience of the small patient, who has the exciting opportunity to have a mother figure all alone five hours a week intently engrossed with him and his ideas and encouraging him to express more'. (Helen Arthur, 'A Comparison of the Techniques Employed in Psychotherapy and Psychoanalysis of Children', *American Journal of Orthopsychiatry*, 22 [1952], pp. 493–4.) I am told by Charlotte Green Schwartz that some male analysts knit or hook rugs during treatment of adult patients, in part, apparently, to divert enough attention to keep themselves from interrupting too frequently.

and delicate feedback control that an individual ordinarily obtains only of and for himself, then, apparently, he must be favorably disposed to the person in command, for such cooperativeness is much easier to win than to exact.[37]

I would like to note here that the chief surgeon may feel obliged to introduce distractions as well as to dispel them. When the spontaneous engagement of the participants in the task activity itself seems likely to tax them too much, the chief surgeon may distract them, for example, by joking. This is just the reverse of the process previously described. Thus, at a point of high tenseness, when a large renal tumor had been completely exposed and was ready to be pierced by a draining needle, a chief surgeon lightly warned before he pierced: 'Now don't get too close.' Another instance of this easing process is found in the fact that the others often seem to look to the chief surgeon to mark the end of a critical phase of action and the beginning of a less critical phase, one that can be used for a general letdown in the sustained concentration of attention and effort. In order to set the tone for these functionally useful relaxations, at the end of a phase of action, the surgeon may stretch himself in a gawky, exaggerated, and clownish way and utter a supportive informality such as 'okey-dokey' or 'th'ar sh' be'. Before the critical phase is begun, and after it has been terminated, he may engage others present in talk about last night's party, the recent ball game, or good places to fish.[38] And when

37. This is nicely illustrated in multi-situated activity systems on board ship, where, it has been claimed, the one time when the captain unbends and uses easy language not ordinarily associated with his role is when an engine steersman must be counted on to respond exquisitely to steering directions from the helm.

By the same logic, however, we should be prepared for the fact that at times the task-management obligations of the individual may force him to draw back to the formal position accorded and exact the full swift measure of his authority, for there are times when a flustered subordinate will be steadied better by a sharp negative sanction than by sympathy.

38. Under strictest possible procedure, no talking would be tolerated except when technically necessary, since germs can apparently be spread through masks in this way. My own experience was in relatively informal hospitals where irrelevant talks and byplays did occur. Burling and Wilson report a similar experience. Presumably the medical traditions of different regions differ in this regard, as suggested by Eugene de Savitsch, *In Search of Complications* (New York: Simon and Schuster, 1940), pp. 374–5: 'In a clinic or operating room almost anywhere in the world all would be silence, soft lights, and sustained tension. In France everybody chatters away as merrily as in a cafe. While a brain tumor, for instance, is removed, the surgeon, his assistants, and the audience – if any – argue over the merits of the present cabinet, disclose the shortcomings of their wives, and exchange advice about stocks and bonds.'

the patient is being closed up and the critical work is quite over, the chief surgeon may initiate and tolerate joking with nurses, bantering with them about their lack of proficiency or about the operation not being nearly over. If no male nurse is present to lift the patient from the operating table to the trolley, the chief surgeon, if he is still in the operating room, may gallantly brush aside the efforts of one of the nurses and insist on lifting the heaviest part of the patient, the middle, himself, acting now in the capacity of a protective male, not a medical person.

Just as the chief surgeon may mark the point where attentiveness may be usefully relaxed, so he, and sometimes others on the team, will put brackets around the central task activity with the result that the level of concern required for it will not be demanded of the team before matters actually get under way and after they have ended. This is nicely shown not merely in the ritual of tearing off one's gloves and immediately leaving the operating room, by which the chief surgeon tells the team that teacher is no longer checking up on them and they can relax, but also in the way in which the body is handled. During the operation, the body of the patient is the rightful focus of a great deal of respectful sustained consideration, technically based, especially in connection with the maintenance of asepsis, blood levels, and respiration. It is as if the body were a sacred object, regardless of the socio-economic character of its possessor, but in this case the consideration given is rational as well as ritual. As might be expected, then, before and after the operation proper there can be observed minor acts of desacralization, whereby the patient is reduced to more nearly profane status. At the beginning of the task the surgeon may beat a tattoo on the leg of the anesthetized patient, and at the end he may irreverently pat the patient on the bottom, commenting that he is now better than new. The surgeon is not alone in this activity. While scrubbing the anesthetized patient, the nurse may lift up a foot by the toe and speak to it: 'You're not sterile, are you?' In moving the now groggy patient from the operating table to the trolley for the trip to the recovery room, the anesthetist, taking charge of this relatively unskilled physical action, may obtain concerted effort from the other persons helping him by saying: 'Ready, aim, fire.' Similarly, in moving an anesthetized patient on his side for a thoracotomy, the anesthetist may say: 'O.K., kids, are we ready to play flip flop? Ready? O.K.'

In addition to maintaining the capacities and poise of other members of the team, the chief surgeon has, of course, an obligation to maintain his own. Moreover, he must be concerned not only with sustaining his own mobilization of personal resources, but also with the anxious attention that other members of the team might give to this. If they feel he is about to lose his temper, or that he has lost his skill, they themselves can become extremely uneasy and inefficient. Thus, when the surgeon runs into trouble that could cause his teammates a distracting and suppressed concern over how he might react to his trouble, we find him engaging in quite standard strategies of tension management, sometimes concealing his own real concerns to do so. He alludes openly to the incident in such a way as to rob it of its capacity to distract the team.[39] When he drops an instrument, he may respond unseriously to his own action by a word such as 'oopsadaisy'. If he must give an order to one of his assistants which might leave the others not knowing if he were angry or not, he may deliver it in a false English accent, in adolescent slang, or in some other insulating way. Unable to find the right spot for a lumbar puncture, he may, after three tries, shake his head a little, as if to suggest that he, as a person sensitive to ideal standards, is still sensitive to them and yet in quiet control of himself, in short, that the implied discrediting of him has not made him lose poise.

Since the chief surgeon's own self-control is crucial in the operation, and since a question concerning it could have such a disquieting effect upon the other members of the team, he may feel obliged to demonstrate that he is in possession of himself, not merely at times of crisis and trouble, but even at times when he would otherwise be silent and so be providing no information one way or the other about his state of mind. Thus, when puzzled about what to do, he may ruminate half out loud, ingenuously allowing others present a close glimpse of his thoughts. During quite delicate tasks, he may softly sing incongruous undignified tunes such as 'He flies through the air with the greatest of ease'. In clamping hemostats, he may let them go from his fingers, flipping them back upon the patient's body in a neat row with the verve and control that parking attendants manifest while parking cars, or merry-go-round managers display in collecting tickets while moving around on the turning platform.

What we have here is a kind of 'externalization' of such feelings and thoughts as are likely to give security and confidence to the other members of the team. This externalization, as well as the constant cut-

39. For a general analysis of this view of tension, see 'Fun in Games', this volume.

ting back of any distractive concern that might have arisen for the team in the course of action, also provides a constant stimulus to team members' attentiveness and task engagement, in both ways helping to hold them to the task as usable participants. Some surgeons, in fact, maintain something of a running line of patter during the operation, suggesting that whenever there is teamwork, someone is likely to have the role function of 'talking it up'.

We see that the chief surgeon is something of a host to persons at his party, as well as the director of his operating team. He is under pressure (however he responds to this pressure) to make sure that those at his table feel good about what is happening so that whatever their capacities they can better exploit them. And to do this morale-maintaining job, at least in America, the surgeon makes use of and draws upon activities not expected of one in his dignified position. When he himself does not perform the clown function, he may encourage someone else, such as the intern or circulating nurse, to take on the job.

In discussing the special responsibilities of the chief surgeon and his frequent need to draw on informality in order to meet these responsibilities, it was implied that the superordinate present may have some special reasons for exhibiting role distance. A further comment should be added concerning the relation between role distance and social ranking.

It seems characteristic of the formalities of a role that adherence to them must be allowed and confirmed by the others involved in the situation; this is one of the basic things we mean by the notion that something is formal and official. Adherence to formalities seems to guarantee the *status quo* of authority and social distance; under the guidance of this style, one can be assured that the others will not be able to move in on one. Reversing the role point of view, we can see that adherence to the formalities one owes to others can be a relatively protective matter, guaranteeing that one's conduct will have to be accepted by the others, and, often, that it will not be difficult to dissociate one's purely covert personal attachments from one's role projection. Finally, it should be added that in general we assume that it is to the advantage of the subordinate to decrease distance from the superordinate and to the advantage of the latter to sustain or increase it.

From these considerations it should be apparent that the exercise of role distance will take on quite different meanings, depending on the relative rank of the individual who exercises it. Should a subordinate exercise role distance, this is likely to be seen as a sign of his refusal to keep his place (thereby moving toward greater intimacy with the superordinate, which the latter is likely to disapprove), or as rejection of authority,[40] or as evidence of low morale. On the other hand, the manifestation of role distance on the part of the superordinate is likely to express a willingness to relax the *status quo*, and this the subordinate is likely to approve because of its potential profitability for him. In the main, therefore, the expression of role distance is likely to be the prerogative of the superordinate in an interaction. In fact, since informality on the part of the inferior is so suspect, a tacit division of labor may arise, whereby the inferior contributes respect for the *status quo* on behalf of both parties, while the superior contributes a glaze of sociability that all can enjoy. Charm and colorful little informalities are thus usually the prerogatives of those in higher office, leading us mistakenly to assume that an individual's social graces helped bring him to his high position, instead of what is perhaps more likely, that the graces become possible for anyone who attains the office.[41] Hence, it is the surgeon, not the surgical nurse, who injects irony into medical etiquette. All of this, it may be added, fits other things we know about relations between unequals. It is the ship's captain who has a right to enter the territory of the ordinary seamen, the 'fo'c'sle', not they to enter his. An officer has a right to penetrate the private life of a soldier serving under him, whereas the private does not have a similar right. In this connection, one student has been led to speak of the social distance between two individuals as being of different extent depending from whose place one starts.[42]

But, of course, subordinates can exercise much role distance, and not merely through grumbling. By sacrificing the seriousness of their

40. For example, I know of a nurse who was transferred from an experimental surgery team, in part because she enacted simulated yawns, meant to be humorous, during the ticklish part of a delicate surgical technique, thereby showing role distance above her station.

41. An empirical illustration of this is presented in an excellent paper by Rose Coser in which she demonstrates the special joking prerogatives of senior psychiatrists during ward meetings; see her 'Laughter Among Colleagues', *Psychiatry*, 23 (1960), pp. 81–95. For further illustrations of role distance on the part of superordinates, see Ralph Turner, 'The Navy Disbursing Officer as a Bureaucrat', *American Sociological Review*, 12 (1947), pp. 342–8.

42. Donald McRae, 'Class Relationships and Ideology', *The Sociological Review*, n.s., 6 (1958), pp. 263–4.

claim to being treated as full-fledged persons, they can exercise liberties not given to social adults.

We can now see that with the chief surgeon on one side and the intern on the other there appears to be a standard distribution of role-distance rights and role-distance tendencies. The intern may sacrifice his character as a full and serious person, becoming, thereby, a half-child in the system, in return for which he is allowed to offend medical role requirements with impunity. The person with dominating status can also offend with impunity because his position gives others present a special reason for accepting the offense.

I would like to add that although the person who manifests much role distance may, in fact, be alienated from the role, still, the opposite can well be true: in some cases only those who feel secure in their attachment may be able to chance the expression of distance. And, in fact, in spite of interns, it appears that conformity to the prescriptive aspects of role often occurs most thoroughly at the neophyte level, when the individual must prove his competence, sincerity, and awareness of his place, leaving the showing of distance from a role to a time when he is firmly 'validated' in that role.

Another peculiarity should be mentioned. To express role-irrelevant idiosyncrasies of behavior is to expose oneself to the situation, making more of oneself available in it than is required by one's role. The executive's family picture on his desk, telling us that he is not to be considered entirely apart from his loved ones, also tells us, in a way, that they are in this occupation with him, and that they might understand his having to work late or open up his house to politically wise sociability.

The differing bases of role distance displayed by the chief surgeon and by the intern imply a division of labor or role differentiation. The nursing personnel exhibit a similar kind of differentiation among themselves: the division of labor and responsibility between the scrub nurse and the circulating nurse is associated with a difference in manifestation of role distance. The scrub nurse, in addition to her continued task obligation during the operation, may feel obliged to maintain the role function of standard-maintainer, policing the aseptic character of the order that is maintained, as well as keeping a Management's eye on the skills of the physicians. Any withdrawal of herself into the role of female might, therefore, jeopardize the situated system. The circulating nurse, on the other hand, has no such responsibilities, and, apparently, these sexual considerations can be displaced onto her. Further, not needing to be 'in' the operation as must the scrub nurse, she can withdraw into herself, or into a conversation with the anesthetist or the nurses in the adjacent operating room, without jeopardizing matters. To place her in a female capacity does not reduce manpower. It is not surprising, therefore, that the circulating nurse, in addition to the intern, is allowed to be flighty – to act without character.

The division of role-function labor that I have described has a characteristic subtlety that should be mentioned again in conclusion. A person with a specialized task not only performs a service needed by the system but also provides a way of being, a selfhood, with which others in the system can identify, thus allowing them to sustain an image of themselves that would disrupt matters if sustained other than vicariously. The 'good guy' informality of the chief surgeon can give his subordinates a feeling that they are not the sort to tolerate strict subordination, that in fact the surgeon must see this and has adjusted himself correspondingly, yet this is, of course, a vicarious rebelliousness carried out principally by the very agency against which one would ordinarily rebel. In the same way, the circulating nurse can establish the principle of female sexuality in which the surgical nurse can see her own reflection, even while the surgeon is calling her by a masculine last-name term of address and receiving a man-sized work contribution from her.

Some final points may now be mentioned concerning the function of role distance, now not merely in surgery but in situated systems in general.

First, by not demanding the full rights of his position, the individual finds that he is not completely committed to a particular standard of achievement; should an unanticipated discrediting of his capacity occur, he will not have committed himself and the others to a hopelessly compromised position. Second, it appears that social situations as such retain some weight and reality in their own right by drawing on role distance – on the margin of reservation the individual has placed between himself and his situated role.

An interesting confirmation of the functional significance of role distance in situated activity systems is to be had by examining situations where roles are played *at*.

There seems to be little difficulty in getting stage actors to portray a character who is inflated with pomposity or bursting with emotion, and directors often have to restrain members of the cast from acting too broadly. The actor is apparently pleased to express before a large audience a lack of reservation which he would probably blush to express off the stage. However, this willingness to embrace a staged role is understandable. Since the actor's performed character is not his real one, he feels no need to safeguard himself by hedging his taken stand. Since the staged drama is not a real one, overinvolvement will simply constitute the following of a script, not a threat to one's capacity to follow it. An acted lack of poise has none of the dysfunctions of real flustering.

More significant, there is the fact that in prisons and mental hospitals, where some inmates may constantly sustain a heroic edifice of withdrawal, uncooperativeness, insolence, and combativeness, the same inmates may be quite ready to engage in theatricals in which they enact excellent portraits of civil, sane, and compliant characters. But this very remarkable turnabout is understandable too. Since the staged circumstances of the portrayed character are not the inmate's real ones, he has no need (in the character's name) to exhibit distance from them, unless, of course, the script calls for it.

A SIMULTANEOUS MULTIPLICITY OF SELVES

It is common in sociology to study the individual in terms of the conception he and others have of him, and to argue that these conceptions are made available to him through the role that he plays. In this paper, the focus of role is narrowed down to a situated activity system. And it is argued that the individual must be seen as someone who organizes his expressive situational behavior *in relation* to situated activity roles, but that in doing this he uses whatever means are at hand to introduce a margin of freedom and maneuverability, of pointed disidentification, between himself and the self virtually available for him in the situation.

Instead, then, of starting with the notion of a definition of the situation we must start with the idea that a particular definition is *in charge of the situation*, and that as long as this control is not overtly threatened or blatantly rejected, much counter-activity will be possible. The individual acts to say: 'I do not dispute the direction in which things are going and I will go along with them, but at the same time I want you to know that you haven't fully contained me in the state of

affairs.' Thus, the person who mutters, jokes, or responds with sarcasm to what is happening in the situation is nevertheless going along
with the prevailing definition of the situation – with whatever bad
spirit. The current system of activity tells us what situated roles will
be in charge of the situation, but these roles at the same time provide
a framework in which role distance can be expressed. Again, it should
be noted that face-to-face interaction provides an admirable context
for executing a double stance – the individual's task actions unrebel-
liously adhere to the official definition of the situation, while gestural
activity that can be sustained simultaneously and yet noninterferingly
shows that he has not agreed to having all of himself defined by what
is officially in progress.

In whatever name the individual exerts role distance, it is plain, by
definition, that the injected identification will be more or less in opposition to the one available in the situated role. But we must now see
that role distance is merely an extreme instance of expressions not a
part of the self virtually available in a role, and that many other, less
opposing, expressions can also occur. As long as the dominion of the
situated role is not challenged, other role identities, ones different
from but not necessarily opposed to the officially available self, can
be sustained too. Role distance directs attention to the fact that situated roles allow for nonrelevant expressions but does not tell us much
about the range of these expressions.

Our problem can now be rephrased. Given a situated role and the
self that virtually awaits the performer and given, too, a range of self-
expression not intrinsically required by this role, what can we say
about the affiliative cross-pressures that seem to arise wherever there
is a situated activity system? What is there about the context in which
these systems are situated that leads systematically to the appearance
of certain alternate identifications?

In the previous section it was suggested that the exigencies of maintaining an activity system themselves develop needs that can be
fulfilled through the exercise of role distance. The chief surgeon's
commitment and attachment to the activity system may override his
immediate concern about maintaining an officially correct stance. If
we revert to the case of the surgical junior, a similar kind of fact
emerges. It was suggested that one source of the young doctor's res-
tiveness in the situation is that he is, after all, a graduated medical
man, and the assistant's situated role may not be of sufficient weight
in his eyes to be consistent with his conception of himself as a doctor.

Here we see a conflict or discrepancy between the self generated in a situated circuit of vital hospital activity and the self associated with a formal status and identity: medical man. No doubt we have here an exaggeration of the kind of discrepancy that can exist between a broad social title and a particular activity system sustained while on duty. Surely in every case, however, there will be *some* discrepancy between the self emerging from a situated activity role and the self associated with the role title in the name of which the activity is carried on. Role distance attests to this discrepancy. One basic limit, then, to embracement of a situated role is the claims of the institutional role in terms of which the participant officially participates. Surgery requires acts unbecoming a surgeon, just as mothering requires acts that are unmaternal. Only where a situated role was not seen as part of a wider institutional complex would the issue not arise.

The next issue to consider is that while an activity system situated in a social establishment may provide a fairly coherent, self-consistent bundle of tasks for a given participant, he will, at the same time, be *officially* involved in other, multi-situated matters that have a relevant claim on his time – a claim that he may be able to honor only by diverting some of the concern that is owed the situated activity. For example, in the many cases where the surgery ward is carrying on some kind of training program, the surgeon directing the operation will periodically halt or slow up the flow of action to instruct the residents and interns in what is happening and about the character of the pathology, its frequency, likely course, and forms of treatment. This benefits surgery in general but neither the particular instance of its application nor the particular patient. Similarly, new techniques may be tested, and ones not used for a long time re-employed, not so much to keep surgery up to the mark but rather the particular surgeon, again to the possible disadvantage of the particular patient. So, too, the surgeon may momentarily check engagement in the task to answer the loudspeaker's request about his plans for next day, or to ask the circulating nurse to phone his office to rearrange some appointments, or he may briefly discuss with the nursing supervisor the effect of the current operation on the ward's schedule for the day. In all these ways in which the individual may properly act as a hospital staff man, he may find that he must express some small distance from the specific operation at hand.

In addition to these task-like claims of a multi-situated kind, there are other claims we must consider that are more purely social in character. In any work establishment, the individual becomes involved in social relationships and group formation. As units of interpersonal solidarity, these may or may not coincide with the boundaries of the various administrative units, such as the establishment itself, divisions within the establishment, and teams formally designated as responsible for specific activity systems. A required administrative action that inhibits the formation of these solidarizing social bonds or threatens bonds already formed may then have to be softened in the interests of solidarity. This softening is often accomplished by means of expressed withdrawal from situated role.

A classic instance of this softening of formal behavior is found in situated activity systems where 'personal' interests have begun to develop. A nice illustration may be taken from a short story by William Sansom, where he describes the protracted and partially successful effort of a man to court a girl he has found serving as a clerk in the garden equipment section of a large store:

Slowly we grew to know one another. I kept a most reserved distance. I bought my seeds and went quickly away – scarcely noticing her, scarcely giving her the usual words of polite encounter . . . I kept my distance – until the day when I judged sincerity to be established and consulted her upon the roller. From then on our acquaintance grew. But not apace. It may sound as if all this were coldly and carefully calculated – but nothing of the sort. My simple hopes were the companions of unbearable terror, of failures of strength and sudden exits, of tentative pleasantries that smothered me as I stammered them – it was then like balancing on some impelling precipice – and I was dogged by an overwhelming distaste for the falsehoods I had to tell. I had, for instance, to invent a garden. But gradually we grew to know each other.

And there were aspects of great charm in our development. When, for instance, I noticed how in her very words she began to change towards me. At first she had spoken to me only in the aloof, impersonal vernacular of gardens. When I enquired how to use an insecticide – I was told that I must 'broadcast among the plants'. About a carton of lime – this must be dusted along the rows of peas to 'hasten pod-filling'. But as time went on and ease overcame her, it was 'just scatter it everywhere' – and 'pod-filling' became 'the peas come quicker'.[43]

Since Mr Sansom's heroine marries another suitor met and cultivated in the same way, she presumably also performed her occupational

43. William Sansom, *A Touch of the Sun* (New York: Reynal & Co., 1958), pp. 54–5.

duties informally for the luckier man, and what Mr Sansom is telling
us is that situated role behavior may be modified not by something
that is intrinsically 'human' or 'personal' but by conduct suitable
for male-female courting relationships, conduct so well formalized
in our society that it can be initiated and sustained between persons
who start out as strangers. In the same way, when a surgeon feels
his assistant has made a strategic blunder, and finds himself bursting
forth in negative sanction of the assistant, he may suddenly inject a
first name or nickname term of address to bolster up the personal
relationship in the face of action that might jeopardize it. He does so
much as a spouse uses the term 'dear' in careful measured tones, to
make sure the entire marital relationship is not threatened by the
sanctioning occurring within it. Again, what we see here is not the
mere reduction of formality but rather an identification with one
type of structure at the expense of another.

Just as the individual must manage his social relationships to his
fellow participants, apart from the role demands of the situated system, so also he gives some concern to his relationships to persons not
present – and this in the face of any assumptions we have about role
segregation. A surgeon may not operate on his wife, as the traditional
arguments about role segregation suggest, and once an operation has
begun he can easily decline to be called to an urgent telephone call
from her or anyone else, but the surgeons I observed wore wedding
rings underneath their rubber gloves, discussed their wives' health
during the operation, and joked with the nurses about being fully
married men. Like the executives I mentioned earlier, some kept in
their clinic offices a picture of wife and children to attest to the fact
that even here, in the citadel of the profession, they had not put their
family entirely away from them. Patients presumably might then be
led to keep in mind that the person they dealt with was something
more than a doctor.

Beginning with our surgical example, we find, more important still,
that there are sources of self-identification such as age and sex cate-
gorization which penetrate the surgical activity system in a diffuse
way, qualifying and modifying conduct where this can be done without threatening the task that controls the situation. Thus, while a surgical nurse may be accorded a last-name term of address, perhaps as
a compliment to, and reinforcement of, her purely technical capacities, her last name is as frequently prefaced by a sexual placement:
'Miss'. Further, female nurses are traditionally excused from 'prep-

ping' the male genitalia, and from having to lift the patient from the
trolley to the operating table and back again. And it is always touching to see, when a patient is on the table and his insides are being
sliced, pried, and tied, that, if the point of incision allows, his private
parts will be carefully kept covered by actions that have decency and
modesty in their style, whether out of respect for him, for the mixture
of sexes that are likely to be present, or for society at large.

Age-sex identifications during task performances typically express
concerns that are felt in addition to the task, not in opposition to it.
Sometimes, however, there is an 'overdetermined' flavor to these
expressions, suggesting that role distance is involved and requiring
the individual to withdraw a little from the occupational game in
order to be momentarily active in the older one:

SCRUB NURSE [*to intern*]: Take one [hemostat] in each hand, he'll need
'em.
INTERN: Yes, Ma-ma.
SCRUB NURSE [*half apologetically*]: I'm really interested in you learn-
ing.
INTERN [*with mock intrigue*]: Well, how about teaching me?
SCRUB NURSE: I gave you a book, what else can I do?
INTERN: Oh there's lots else you can do.
SCRUB NURSE [*to Chief Surgeon*]: Do you want me here or on the other
side?
INTERN [*next to whom she had been standing*]: Stay here close to me.

I would like to add that it would be wrong indeed to overestimate the
sexuality of these sexual references. They resemble a tickle much more
than a caress. Sex here seems to be made a convenience of, seized
upon not for itself but to demonstrate a little independence regarding
one's situated role. If serious at all, these joking remarks allow the
surgeon to stake a claim to roles he might want to be available to him
at another time and in another setting.

Although it is obvious that principles of identity and social organization such as age and sex are always receiving their small due, the
reason why we have not constructed an approach that gives appropriate place to them is not as apparent. Perhaps our concern about
prejudice and discrimination – the introduction of bases of identity
that we feel ought not to have been introduced – has led us to see all
this play of identification around the central task theme as a kind of
illegitimate and unfortunate deviation from the norm – a particularistic invasion of sacred universalistic ground. In fact, of course, to

embrace a situated role fully and exclusively is more the exception than the rule.

I have argued that the individual does not embrace the situated role that he finds available to him while holding all his other selves in abeyance. I have argued that a situated activity system provides an arena for conduct and that in this arena the individual constantly twists, turns, and squirms, even while allowing himself to be carried along by the controlling definition of the situation. The image that emerges of the individual is that of a juggler and synthesizer, an accommodator and appeaser, who fulfils one function while he is apparently engaged in another; he stands guard at the door of the tent but lets all his friends and relatives crawl in under the flap. This seems to be the case even in one of our most sacred occupational shows – surgery.

I have also argued that these various identificatory demands are not created by the individual but are drawn from what society allots him. He frees himself from one group, not to be free, but because there is another hold on him. While actively participating in an activity system, he is, nevertheless, also obliged to engage in other matters, in relationships, in multi-situated systems of activity, in sustaining norms of conduct that crosscut many particular activity systems. I want now to try to look more closely at some of the cultural influences that seem to be at work determining the expression of role-irrelevant identifications during role performance – influences that are broadly based in the society at large, in spite of the narrow arena in which they are given their due.

Given the fact that a man in the role of surgeon must act at times during surgery like a male, the question arises as to what capacity he is active in, what role he is playing, when he decides how to allocate his time and action between these two roles.

We find a clue when we examine the rules for beginners, whatever is being learned. When an individual is first working into his role, he will be allowed to approach his tasks diffidently, an excuse and apology ready on his lips. At this time he is likely to make many otherwise discreditable mistakes, but for this time he has a learner's period of grace in which to make them – a period in which he is not yet quite the person he will shortly be, and, therefore, cannot badly damage himself by the damaging expression of his maladroit actions. In the medical world, of course, this temporary license is institutionalized in the statuses of intern and junior resident. Here, incumbents have sufficiently little face to allow of their being scolded by senior staff and twitted by nurses, in that important arrangement by which children and others in training are permitted to pay for their mistakes in cash on the spot, thereby avoiding certain kinds of liens on their future.

While it is possible to say that the surgeon's role makes allowance for maladroitness in beginners, we might just as economically argue that in our society there is a general appreciation that the individual, as a role-performer, ought to be given time to learn, and that the time thus given young surgeons expresses our conception of role-taker, not surgeon. If the sociologist can see past the particularities of a specific occupation to the general theme of the learner's plight, then perhaps society can too.

Roles certainly differ according to how seriously and fully the performers must stick to the script. Even in the most serious of roles, such as that of surgeon, we yet find that there will be times when the full-fledged performer must unbend and behave simply as a male. In the same way, we have strict rules about how lightly the individual can treat an occupational role, and we know that boxers and baseball players who mock their role may be seriously sanctioned. Given a range of occupations, then – the professions, say – we find general understandings as to how stiff and how loose the performer may be. I think we can argue that these norms of seriousness do not always attach to our image of particular callings and persons performing in them, but rather to wider groupings of roles and even to role-enactment as such. To generalize, then, one could say that a role-performer in our society has a right to some learner's license and a limit to formality of obligation – by sheer virtue of being a role-taker.

Since norms regarding the management of one's multiple identifications derive in part from the general culture, we should expect differences in this regard from society to society, and this is certainly the case. Throughout Western society, segregative tendencies as regards role are strong, and it is often expected that a person active in a given occupational or organizational role will not subvert his responsibilities there in favor of other ties, such as familial ones, while in Eastern societies there is less of this kind of compartmentalization.

Even within Western society we may expect some differences. In British society, for example, in the recent past, the ideology of influential classes focused on the amateur player – the gentleman politician, the gentleman scholar, and the gentleman explorer. There was an anti-commercial hope that the individual would become a 'rounded person', not given over in a warped, constraining way to one calling. The ideal, apparently, was to exert high skill diffidently, a shark got up in bumbler's clothing. American society, by contrast, seems to have licensed a greater bustling in one's occupational role – anger, haste, sleeves rolled up, and other signs of full engagement in the moment's task. (Perhaps we can even point to changes in style in this regard: the Madison Avenue complex seems to be associated with a decline in role segregation, accompanied by the soft sell and by very friendly office relations across status levels.) But even in our own society, role distance abounds, occurring in many contexts, with many functions, and in response to many motives.

There is other evidence that points in the direction of our having conceptions of role-taking as such. In every establishment where roles are institutionalized, some limitations on duty will also be institutionalized. Working conditions are regulated with a view to preservation of health; time off is given for eating, rest, and recreation. In some sense it is not a nurse or an orderly that warrants these privileges, but a person or citizen, and it is in part by virtue of this pervasive qualification that these rights are extended.[44]

Further, there is the extremely interesting institution of 'extenuating circumstances'. A man at work should tend to his job and forget about his family. Yet even in the most demanding of workplaces, it is recognized that the person who is a worker does have these other role concerns and that when he is in a state of crisis regarding them he should be allowed some time off from the legitimate work claims which ordinarily can be made on him. A soldier whose wife is having a child may be given some leave, as may an executive. I suggest that it is not as a soldier or an executive that the person gets leave, nor merely as a husband and father, but rather in part as a multiple-role-player who can compartmentalize himself within limits but who cannot, according to our conceptions of him, be asked to go too far in this compartmentalization.

In all these cases we see that the individual limits the degree to which he embraces a situated role, or is required to embrace it, because of society's understanding of him as a multiple-role-performer rather than as a person with a particular role. This view of the individual, which empties his particular role of all content and conceives

44. T. H. Marshall, *Citizenship and Social Class* (Cambridge University Press, 1950), pp. 1–85.

of him, formally, as a person of many identifications, whatever these particular identifications are, is expressed in still other ways.[45] Just as the surgeon is expected to remember today what happened at the clinic yesterday, so also, should he meet his wife in the hospital, he may be excused from operating on her, but nothing will excuse him from greeting her. In fact, we have extensive institutions of greeting whereby two individuals who are not then going to be involved together in an undertaking acknowledge that they will, or may be, so involved at other times. Finally, in a dim way we have conceptions of the limited and compensatory character of human attachment, and, whether justifiably or not, we try to understand the distance a man seems to maintain from his job by the closeness of his attachment to a hobby.

In summary, then, it may be stated that, given a situated system as a point of reference, role distance is a typical, not normative, aspect of role. But the lightness with which the individual handles a situated role is forced upon him by the weight of his manifold attachments and commitments to multi-situated social entities. Disdain for a situated role is a result of respect for another basis of identification.

When we shift our point of reference from the situated system, then, to these wider entities, role distance can again be seen as a response to a normative framework. As far as merry-go-round riding is concerned, the role distance exhibited by an eight-year-old boy is a typical, not obligatory, part of the situation; for the boy's manhood, however, these expressions are obligatory. A statistical departure in the first case would be a moral departure in the second.

CONCLUSIONS

Much role analysis seems to assume that once one has selected a category of person and the context or sphere of life in which one wants to consider him, there will then be some main role that will fully dominate his activity. Perhaps there are times when an individual does march up and down like a wooden soldier, tightly rolled up in a

45. Much of our legal framework, which imputes individual responsibility, deals with the individual as an historically continuous, uniquely identifiable entity, and not as a person-in-role or a person as a set of role-slices. A financial debt incurred in one sphere of life while active in one capacity will have to be paid by monies drawn from what is due to others.

particular role. It is true that here and there we can pounce on a moment when an individual sits fully astride a single role, head erect, eyes front, but the next moment the picture is shattered into many pieces and the individual divides into different persons holding the ties of different spheres of life by his hands, by his teeth, and by his grimaces. When seen up close, the individual, bringing together in various ways all the connections that he has in life, becomes a blur. Hence many who have analyzed roles have stood across the street from the source of their data, oriented by William James's abstract view of human action instead of by the lovingly empirical view established by his younger brother.[46]

One can limit oneself to a particular category of persons in a particular context of life – a situated role in a situated activity system – but no matter how narrow and specific these limits, one ends up by watching a dance of identification. A surgeon does not bring his wife to the operating table and is not in a husbandly relation to the body that is his patient, but it does not follow that while in the surgical theater he acts solely in the capacity of a surgeon. I suppose one might want to ask what a salesgirl does in a store by virtue of her being a salesgirl. The test of close analysis, however, is to study what a person who is a salesgirl does in a store that persons who are not salesgirls do not do, for much of what only salesgirls do in stores is not done by them *qua* salesgirls and has nothing to do with sales. Thus, as a student[47] has recently shown, waitresses in British dock canteens can find that self-applied norms on the job refer to extra-work relations with male customers, these norms being finally understandable only in terms of the general values of the community in which the canteens are located. What is necessitated here, then, is a fundamental shift from Linton's *stated* point of view: we do not ask how a chief surgeon, *qua* surgeon, is expected to act during surgery, but how those individuals who are designated chief surgeon are expected to act during surgery.

46. Instances of microscopic analysis are to be found in R. G. Barker and H. F. Wright, *One Boy's Day* (New York: Harper, 1951), and, sometimes beautifully, in the occasional pieces of Ray Birdwhistell. See also the remarkable paper by Donald Roy, '"Banana Time": Job Satisfaction and Informal Interaction', *Human Organization*, 18 (Winter, 1959–60), pp. 158–68. 'Small group' experimenters have certainly stood up close to their data but have used a considerable amount of this opportunity to adjust their equipment.

47. E. M. Mumford, 'Social Behaviour in Small Work Groups', *The Sociological Review*, n.s., 7 (1959), pp. 137–57.

Further, a broadened version of Linton's role conceptions allows us to distinguish typical role from normative role and to treat role distance as something that can be typical and not normative. We can then, for example, deal with the pin-ups that workers and soldiers attach to their locker doors, noting that these posters introduce a thin layer of sex between what the men define themselves as and what the institutional scene has defined them as. We can see that not only a sexual stimulus is involved but also a moral wedge, the same kind that is employed by middle-class boys who separate themselves from their familial environment by hanging purloined stop signs and other emblems of civic irreverence in their bedrooms.

Furthermore, once role is broadened and attention is directed to role distance, we can deal with ranges of data that were ill-suited to traditional role analysis. I provide some graduated examples.

Starting with an individual's situated role in a situated system of activity, we can proceed to the domain traditionally handled by role analysis by assuming that his situated role is entirely characteristic of (and a reflection of) his role in a social establishment, an occupational system, a formal organization in which the situated system has its institutional setting. As suggested earlier, the terms needed in order to deal with the facts of behavior within a situated system can then be extended *pari passu* to roles in any kind of multi-situated setting.

But this movement from situated systems to social establishments need no longer take us to the limits of the domain to which role concepts can be applied. So-called 'diffuse' or conditioning roles, such as age-sex roles, can now be considered, too, even though we can only point to modulations they introduce in the performance of other roles and can point neither to social establishments in which they have their principal jurisdiction nor to any bundle of tasks allocated to the performer. So also we can now include even more loosely structured roles arising in connection with such items as physical appearance, attainments of skill and education, city of residence, relations to particular others, group affiliations of many kinds. Their inclusion is important, for each of these facts can place the individual in a life situation from which he might draw an identification of self and from which he might seek some distance, even though no coherent set of obligations and expectations – no social role in the traditional sense – may be involved.

Clothing patterns provide a systematic example for analysis with a broadened conception of role and illustrate the way in which the phenomenon of role distance requires our adopting this view. Young psychiatrists in state mental hospitals who are sympathetic to the plight of patients sometimes express distance from their administrative medical role by affecting shirts open at the collar, much as do socialists in their legislative offices. Housemaids willing to wear a uniform but not to confine their hair by a cap provide a parallel example, partially rejecting their occupation in favor of their femininity.[48] (What we have in these cases is a special kind of status symbol – a disidentifier – that the individual hopes will shatter an otherwise coherent picture, telling others not what he is but what he isn't quite.) However, it is not only organizational roles which are handled in this way. Age-sex roles are dealt with in the same manner, as when a girl dresses in a tomboy style, or a sixty-year-old man wears the brim of his hat turned up or affects a crewcut. A vivid example of this kind of disidentifier may be cited in regard to 'race' groupings, taken from a novelistic description of the functions of clothing for a New York Negro, very hip, by name of Movement:

The tension had got bad right after he left Kiefer. It had been all right in Harlem – there he had been staging his own entrances and exits, no involvement, it was an elaborate game, like most of existence up there. But at the tailor's when he found the shoulder pads had not been removed from his jacket, he began to tighten up, his gut establishing dangerous liaison with his face.

'To know what kind of shoulders I want', he said, his voice twice as colorless as usual, 'you would have to know who I am, or who I want to be. Who would know that better, you or me?'

'So who are you?' the tailor said. 'Jimmy Stewart? Anthony Eden?'

'You do not understand. What is this suit you make over and over, with the padded shoulders and the extreme drape and the pegged trousers? A uniform, Sam. I do not want to wear a uniform. Uniforms are for people who want to show themselves, not for those who want to hide.'

'Movement, you're crazy. You don't like uniforms, all right. But you think this pogo-stick garment ain't a uniform? You look at those advertising guys marching on Madison, all look-alikes with buttondown collars, all

48. Sexual attractiveness provides an exemplary means of role distance for females in the work world and is certainly not restricted to females in the meaner callings. For example, there is a tacit understanding in the medical world that female physicians on hospital staffs will mute their attractiveness (where they have any). A highly placed, good-looking female physician is therefore in a position, sometimes utilized, to bring a little pleasant uneasiness to an entire hospital.

they need is a top sergeant yelling the march orders at them. It's a uniform like Cab Calloway's white gabardine reet-pleat is a uniform, only it's thin and up-and-down and the other one it's wide and sideways and curvy more.'

'It is a uniform', Movement said, 'to those who wear it as a uniform. To the Madison Avenue people. For me, it is a disguise, to get the eyes off me.'

'Disguise, schmisguise. So you wear also a gold earring? That's a disguise too?'

'Between the earring and the Brooks Brothers suit', Movement said, lips fighting to keep down the shout that was accumulating, 'is where I am. Where they stop crowding me. I have some elbow room there and that is my freedom.'[49]

But of course we cannot stop with organizational, age-sex, and ethnic group roles. A person of wealth may affect poor and worn clothing for many reasons, one of which is to demonstrate that he is something apart from what his wealth allows him to be. And what his wealth allows him is not a situated role in any full sense of the term, but rather a human situation in which certain contingencies are likely. In the same way, we would have to deal with the appearance pattern affected among bohemians, through which they expressively take a stand against that quite amorphous social entity – middle-class society.

The move from closely meshed situated systems to loose bases for roles is not the only one we must make. The role distance exhibited even in a situated system cannot itself always be handled as I have so far suggested. In some cases, as with the antics of merry-go-round riders and surgeons, role distance clearly seems to express a measure of disidentification relative to the identification available to anyone in the given situated position. It is soon apparent, however, that this distance may be meant to be seen as symbolic of distance from something different than position in the situated activity circuit. The individual may actually be attempting to express some disaffiliation from his position in a different kind of entity – a social relationship

49. Bernard Wolfe, *The Late Risers* (New York: Random House, 1954), pp. 217–18. The expressive significance of wearing only *one* earring is developed in the section called 'grandfather was an authentic field hand', pp. 136–42. For an interesting statement regarding the sartorial role distance of young drug users, see Harold Finestone, 'Cats, Kicks, and Color', *Social Problems*, 5 (1957), pp. 3–13, especially p. 3. See also T. H. Pear, *Personality, Appearance and Speech* (London: Allen and Unwin, 1957), p. 66: 'In World War I, an attempt to compel subalterns to grow a moustache, resulted at times in a defiant cultivation of a dot of hair under each nostril . . .'

that he has to a fellow participant; the social establishment[50] or the social occasion in which the activity system occurs; the professional or occupational world to which the individual belongs.

For example, meal-taking in domestic establishments provides a situated system from which a member of the household may show distance by sitting down late, putting his nose in a book, talking to no one while eating, making 'unmannerly' noises, rejecting all food, or, as in the case of some persons at the onset of what is called a psychotic break, smearing the food or stealing it from the plates of others. Now, while such a person is clearly showing distance from the situated role of family meal-taker in a family meal, he may be motivated by an irritation not with the eater's role but with quite different matters – a spouse or parent, his job, the educational system, his girlfriend, the middle-class way of life, and so forth. Another clear example is provided again by surgeons. Often, surgeons make use of a hospital through a staffing arrangement by which they bring in paying patients in exchange for use of surgical facilities and hospital beds. In this bargain, surgeons often seem to feel that the hospital is not providing them with adequate staffing and equipment. During surgery, humorous and sarcastic remarks will thus be passed by surgeons, often to the permanent hospital staff such as nurses and anesthetists, through which the physicians give evidence that while they must accept hospital conditions they are not happy with what they must tolerate.

CHIEF SURGEON [*using the nurse as a target to express joking, hectoring hostility toward management for the inadequacies of the services they lay on*]: Are all my instruments here, Nurse? Is everything I need here, eh? They don't have everything here, I have to bring my own, you know, and I want them back.

And, as implied in the quotation, in order to convey this attitude, surgeons sometimes draw on their store of conduct that is slightly unbecoming to a surgeon.

Given the fact that an individual may employ his role in a situated system to express distance from a basis of self-identification not offi-

50. Very nice instances of this may be found in the language of derision that amputees and brain-surgery cases employ in regard to the hospital and staff involved in their treatment. See Edwin Weinstein and Robert Kahn, *Denial of Illness* (Springfield: Charles Thomas, 1955). For similar joking by patients in mental hospitals, see Rose Coser, 'Some Social Functions of Laughter', *Human Relations*, 12 (1959), pp. 171–82.

cially at issue, we can appreciate that a situated role may be selected
with this in mind. Participation in the situated activity may be made
a convenience of, carried on not for its own sake but for what can
be expressed through it about something else. At the same time, the
individual may mobilize so much of his talk, appearance, and activity
to exhibit distance from a particular role that the role itself may
cease to be visible. All these elements seem to be illustrated in an
interview quoted in a recent paper on the self-hate of intellectual
academics:

When I'm away from the university, I usually have plenty of dirt under
my nails, or I'm getting a harvest. Some of us fool ourselves into believing
that the stain of our profession doesn't follow us. I can work with a car-
penter for several weeks, and he has no notion I'm a university professor.
I take a foolish pride, I suppose, in this.[51]

I suggest, then, that a single framework of analysis must cover the
situation of the person with a traditional, well-focused, task-oriented
role, like that of surgeon, and persons in the situation of being a rich
widower of fifty, a fat girl of bad complexion, a stutterer, and so forth.
And I imply that our actual interest in persons with well-focused roles
has often been such as to render this broader treatment easy and
natural. In cases of both focused and unfocused roles, the basic
interest is in what befalls an individual by virtue of his being in a
position, and whether this position is a part of a tightly encircled system of situated activity or merely the common feature of a heterogeneous class of social situations is not the first issue. Further, even
when we deal with an apparently well-focused role, such as that of
nurse or surgeon, we find that some of the most significant features of
the position arise not while 'on the job' but at times when the individual is officially active in another role, such as that of fellow guest
or motorist. Source of identification is one thing, an audience for this
self-identification is another. Occupational roles with the firmest
grasp on their performers are often ones which carry identifying
implications for the performer when he is off duty and away from the
immediate arena of his role. Often, it is precisely these unfocused
consequences of a focused role that carry much of the reward and

51. Melvin Seeman, 'The Intellectual and the Language of Minorities',
American Journal of Sociology, 64 (1958), p. 32. A recent novel by Mark Harris,
Wake Up, Stupid! (New York: Knopf, 1959), provides a rather full catalogue
of role-distance fantasies for college teachers. The *genre* was, of course, established by Kingsley Amis's *Lucky Jim*.

punishment of playing it – the situations of the policeman, the country nurse, and the minister are examples. One might almost argue that role-formation occurs to the degree that performance of a situated task comes to have significance for the way the performer is seen in other situations, and that the social psychology of identification moves always from a situated system in which a situated role is performed to wider worlds in which the mere fact of this performance comes to carry significance. This is so even though as one moves outward and away from the situated system and its immediate audience of participants, the role term by which the individual is identified may become more and more abstract, a chest man becoming a surgeon, a surgeon a doctor, a doctor a professional man.

I have argued that the individual manifests role distance and less 'counter-oriented' role-irrelevant acts because of the commitments and attachments that he possesses and that these are a heterogeneous lot: his organizational roles, his diffuse roles, the situated system of activity itself. And now I am arguing that another complication is involved. For just as the individual manifests distance (in whatever name) from his situated role, so, too, he spends some of his moments and gestures manifesting distance from some of his non-situated, non-relevant connections.[52]

As regards embracement, then, a person's conduct is complex indeed. Should he happen to be engaged, at the moment of analysis, in a situated role, then this will provide a focus, but rarely a sharp one. The substance of task activity can be more or less restricted to a situated role, but the style, manner, and guise in which this task is performed cannot be thus restricted. Individuals are almost always free to modulate what they are required to do, being free, thus, to give way to the wider constraints of their multiple self-identifications.[53]

52. For a similar view of interaction, see Anselm Strauss, *Mirrors and Masks* (Glencoe: The Free Press, 1959), pp. 56–7.

53. Role distance, Edward Sapir might have suggested, is to role as fashion is to custom: 'Fashion is a custom in the guise of departure from custom. Most normal individuals consciously or unconsciously have the itch to break away in some measure from a too literal loyalty to accepted custom. They are not fundamentally in revolt from custom but they wish somehow to legitimize their personal deviation without laying themselves open to the charge of insensitiveness to good taste or good manners. Fashion is the discreet solution of the subtle conflict. The slight changes from the established in dress or other forms of behavior seem for the moment to give the victory to the individual, while the fact that one's fellows revolt in the same direction gives one a feeling of adventurous safety . . .

One great theme of social organization is the scheduling of roles: the individual is allowed and required to be one thing in one setting and another thing in a different setting, the role that is given primacy at one occasion being dormant on another. In acclaiming this role-segregation, however, sociologists have neglected another basic theme. A situated system of activity and the organization in which this system is sustained provide the individual with that one of his roles that will be given principal weight on this occasion. But even while the local scene establishes what the individual will mainly be, many of his other affiliations will be simultaneously given little bits of credit.

A final comment is to be added. There is a vulgar tendency in social thought to divide the conduct of the individual into a profane and sacred part, this version of the distinction strangely running directly contrary to the one Durkheim gave us. The profane part is attributed to the obligatory world of social roles; it is formal, stiff, and dead; it is exacted by society. The sacred part has to do with 'personal' matters and 'personal' relationships – with what an individual is 'really' like underneath it all when he relaxes and breaks through to those in his presence. It is here, in this personal capacity, that an individual can be warm, spontaneous, and touched by humor. It is here, regardless of his social role, that an individual can show 'what kind of a guy he is'. And so it is, that in showing that a given piece of conduct is part of the obligations and trappings of a role, one shifts it from the sacred category to the profane, from the fat and living to the thin and dead. Sociologists *qua* sociologists are allowed to have the profane part; sociologists *qua* persons, along with other persons, retain the sacred for their friends, their wives, and themselves.

The concept of role distance helps to combat this touching tendency to keep a part of the world safe from sociology. For if an individual is to show that he is a 'nice guy' or, by contrast, one much less nice than a human being need be, then it is through his using or not using role distance that this is likely to be done. It is right here, in manifestations of role distance, that the individual's personal style is to be found. And it is argued in this paper that role distance is almost as much subject to role analysis as are the core tasks of roles themselves.

The endless rediscovery of the self in a series of petty truancies from the official socialized self becomes a mild obsession of the normal individual in any society in which the individual has ceased to be a measure of the society itself.' 'Fashion', *Encyclopedia of the Social Sciences* (New York: Macmillan, 1931), 6, pp. 140–41.